ACKNOWLEDGMENTS

This book is dedicated to my wife Gloria, and my friends and colleagues who inspired me to put my thoughts to print. My special thanks to Ira, Brian, and Smalley, their contribution was invaluable to the creation of this story. I must also acknowledge the one man who gave life to the BLACK KNIGHTS from a conversation he and I had in May 1991 at a symposium that was held in Chicago, Illinois, USA, he was Commander of all Luftwaffe Fighters during World War II, Fieldmarshal Adolf Galland (19 March 1912–9 February 1996). During the War he was one of the top aces with 102 confirmed victories.

BLACK HERITAGE IN WORLD HISTORY

Mother Africa, the largest continent on earth, home to millions of people, the descendants of great civilizations and their heritage dating back to antiquity. Recent history details the occupation and the colonization of this continent by the major nations of Europe and the lucrative slave trade that caused many of these descendants to be forcibly abducted and transported to other lands. Eventually over a period of time after the secession of slavery and the two great wars, World War I and World War II, these African descendants assimilated into the populations of their abductors and adopted the majority of their cultures.

There has become a pilgrimage of African descendants returning to Mother Africa to seek knowledge of their heritage, to educate themselves on their history, to find their roots.

The author has been passionate about pursuing the answers to his own African heritage from an early age as a boy while attending school. The author's path took an unexpected turn and sent him to Germany as a soldier in the United States Army during the closing period of World War II and 25 years later, another extensive journey to Germany. The author's quest for answers to many questions of that great conflict led to the delving into its history and its aftermath. The author found very little mention in the history of this great conflict about African descendants participating in the fighting of this great conflict even though it has been acknowledged that they did fight and did participate. This fictionalized story is the author's contribution to add to the legendary World War II and its aftermath.

Printed in the United States of America on acid-free paper.
15   14   13   3   2   1

Library of Congress Control Number:
ISBN 13: 978-0-910671-06-4

Library of Congress Cataloging-in-Publication Data
Burke, Marcellus J.
    The Black Knights

ISBN 978-0-910671-06-4 (alk. paper)
 1. World War, 1939-1945--Aerial operations, German.
2. Fighter pilots--Germany--Biography. 3.World War, 1939-1945--Campaigns. 4. World War, 1939-1945--Blacks--Germany.
5. Germany. Luftwaffe--Biography. I. Title.
D787.B79 2014
940.54'494308996--dc23
2013046681

Cover photo credit: Crowood Press

Interior illustration credit: Roshawn Allen

Lufthansa Airbus 300 image credit: Arco Publishing

Designer: Solomohn N. Ennis-Klyczek.

CONTENTS

Preface

This book, THE BLACK KNIGHTS, is a story about the lives of four German aviators of African descent who became Luftwaffe pilots during World War II. They fought valiantly and courageously for Germany during the entire war, from 1 September 1939 until Germany's unconditional surrender on 8 May 1945. Their exploits in the air war became legendary, as were the 'mounts' they used. Three of the pilots were fighter pilots, their mounts were primarily the Messerschmitt BF109 fighter, armed with 12.5mm machine guns and the engine mounted 20mm cannon, commonly referred to as the Me109, and the Focke Wulf 190A fighter, or the 'Butcher Bird', armed with 20mm cannons and 12.5mm machine guns. These fighters were among the best in the world during World War II.

One of the pilots became a dive-bomber pilot; he flew the Junkers, Ju87 Sturzkampfflugzeug, or the 'STUKA' dive-bomber. This plane flew on every front during the entire war. The 'STUKA', a terror weapon that included sirens mounted to its undercarriage. The sirens had the nickname, the "Trumpets of Jericho", causing panic to enemy troops below, as they were being bombed and strafed. When this plane was converted to the role of 'tank killer' by adding twin PAK 37mm cannons to its armament, it became one of the most feared planes on the battle fields, most notably in the battles on the Eastern Front in Russia. This pilot later flew the twin-engine Messerschmitt 110 fighter-bomber, often referred to as 'der Zerstorer', or 'the Destroyer' armed with a cluster of two 30mm cannons and four 12.5mm machine guns in the nose and twin 7.92mm machine guns mounted in the rear turret.

These pilots, with their daredevil tactics, combined with their uncanny skills and the mastery of their mounts, and their unwavering tenacity of pressing home their attacks, these four Luftwaffe pilots became known to friend and foe alike as THE BLACK KNIGHTS! Each of them in the beginning of the war had fought on different fronts, in different squadrons. The invasion of Russia on 22 June 1941, known as 'Operation Barbarossa', found these pilots eventually serving exclusively on the Eastern Front in Russia.

It has been noted by historians, such as Delroy Constantine-Simms, delving into Hitler's Germany, and documentaries, such as the film entitled: "Hitler's Forgotten Victims", that some Germans of African descent had been interred in concentration camps and had suffered the same fate as Jews, Gypsies, and other minorities as the war progressed. This news was vigorously suppressed by the Nazis but rumors persisted as these stories circulated throughout Germany. This novel brings to the reader one example of the many unpublished stories of World War II, the participation of Luftwaffe pilots of African descent flying in the hostile skies over Europe and Russia during the greatest conflict in human history!

Chapter

I

The Origin of Each of
the Black Knights

The BLACK KNIGHTS, Leutnants Hans Thayer, Otto Olagande, Charles Toulon, and Max Ule were strangers to each other at the beginning of the war but fate brought them together as the war progressed. Their beginnings from birth until they entered the war were divergent for the exception that all four were descendants of natives of Africa. This is their story.

Hans Thayer was born March 1920 in the small farming town of Neundettelsau, Germany. Hans' father, Karl Thayer, was a native of Togoland, Africa, who joined the French Foreign Legion to escape the life of becoming a slave in his native land. During World War I Karl fought against Germany. After the war's victorious conclusion for the French and her allies, Karl's legionnaires occupied the region of Alsace-Lorraine, a disputed area between France and Germany. There Karl met a pretty German farm girl, Marie Holz, and after several liaisons the couple were married and eventually relocated to the town of Neundettelsau, Germany.

Karl and Marie acquired a few acres of farmland and harvested wheat and oats. Together they worked very hard, putting in long hours, like every other farmer, to help contribute to the food supply of the hungry population of a beleaguered Germany that was recovering from the Great Depression that had ravaged so many other nations around the world. Soon, Karl and Marie were blessed with the birth of their first born, a son, Hans. As soon as Hans became old enough he joined his parents in the fields performing the various chores to help bring in the crops. As Germany's economy began to improve, Karl was able to hire adult farm workers that allowed Karl and Marie to enroll Hans in school. Hans was an average student in academics but he excelled in all the school sports. Hans was powerfully built due to the long laborious hours he spent working in the fields with his parents. Hans represented his school at the local sports events, he entered the gymnastic contests and the wrestling meets, his favorites. Hans won many honors and trophies for the gymnastic contests. Hans' reputation grew and his school sent him to compete in the gymnastic contests being held in Nuremberg.

Hans was a handsome lad with dark wavy hair, deep dark brown eyes, a broad nose and skin the color of bronze. Hans had a winning smile and friendly personality that made him popular with his peers. When Hans first arrived in Nuremberg, he became a curiosity in the eyes of many of the other athletes that had come to the events from other parts of Germany. Hans was the main topic of discussion among the girls that were in attendance, the girls were in awe of this physical specimen with the bronze skin and winning smile, to the dismay of all the other males. Behind the scenes there were many questions concerning Hans' racial and ethnic identity, mainly by the older adults. As Hans won contest after contest his popularity grew and he became the toast of the event. Hans received invitations to all the parties and other gatherings, he wrote his parents telling of all his experiences and the wonderful time he was having. Hans also wrote how he enjoyed the surroundings of the big city of Nuremberg and all the new friends he had acquired. At the conclusion of the event, Hans' school team attended a flying circus performance that had come to Nuremberg. This would become a defining moment in the life of Hans Thayer!

The flying circuses, with their barnstorming pilots performing feats of aerial gymnastics in their flimsy aircraft fascinated Hans to the extent that he became mesmerized by their fantastic stunts. Most of the these aviators were former fighter pilots from World War I, doing their death defying acts for the enjoyment of the audiences below, and for Hans in particular! On his return to Neundettelsau, Hans would imagine himself being in one of those planes performing acrobatics to defy any stunts that the world had ever seen! When Hans arrived home he confided in his father that he would embark on the career of his life, not that of a farmer, but that of an aviator, a dare-devil stunt pilot in a flying circus, performing stunts before huge audiences around the world.

After Hans completed his primary school training, he bid his parents farewell and was off to join a flying circus. Hans started out as a handy man, then he became a mechanic, and after being taught to fly, he tested the planes before the performances. Whenever there was a lull in the flying circus performances Hans would take one of the aircraft aloft and test his skills as a stunt pilot. Hans became so proficient he caught the eye of one of the leading flying circus performers, a former World War I 'ace', Count Frederick von Klaussner. Under the tutelage of the Count, Hans became a leading stunt flyer and performed under the title, 'Der Schwarz Adler' or 'The Black Eagle'.

At this time, Germany was clandestinely rebuilding her air force into the mighty Luftwaffe. Recruiters attended these shows with the expressed purpose of recruiting the top prospects for induction into the Luftwaffe. Count von Klaussner personally recommended to his contacts within the recruiters organization that Hans be considered for induction into the Luftwaffe. The Count was aware that there would be those recruiters who would believe the Luftwaffe was such an elite branch of the services that only applicants considered as 'Pure Aryan' should be inducted. The Count believed that only the best aviators should be inducted into the Luftwaffe, nothing else mattered.

After receiving his orders to report for flight training Hans could not find the words to express his thanks to his mentor and friend, the Count. The reality of performing on the world stage as a fighter pilot surpassed any of Hans' dreams of a few years earlier.

Otto Olagande was born January 1919 in the German colony of Cameroon, Africa. Otto, the son of Otto Knoll Sr., a German diplomatic courier attached to the German embassy in Cameroon and to Princess Tikwana Olagande, daughter of King Nkuno Olagande, Chief of all the Ubo. The Ubo are one of the more progressive tribes in Cameroon, many of their young men travel to the continent of Europe and to England to study at the universities. Many returned to Africa as doctors, teachers, engineers, government employees, and military aides. After the German surrender at the conclusion of World War I, Germany was stripped of her African colonies, which included Cameroon and Togoland. The German embassy staff in Cameroon, which included Otto Knoll, was returned to Germany. The German nationals, mostly the plantation owners, elected to stay in Cameroon, maintaining their land and culture. They lived in the compounds, which were walled cities within the tribal territories. Princess Tikwana and her infant son, Otto, continued to live within the German compound located in the territory of the Ubo. As Otto became older, he was enrolled in the schools within the compound. Otto was never permitted to go outside the confines of the compound, his only contacts and friends were the German children and the few Ubo children of the servants living within the compound. Otto's contact with the Ubo children however was very limited because they were aware he was the grandson of King Nkuno.

King Nkuno persuaded his daughter to return to the tribal lands with her son and raise him according to the

tribal laws and customs of the Ubo. Upon their arrival, deep within the interior of Cameroon, Otto took on the surname of his grandfather, Olagande, and was permitted to sit alongside his grandfather and the Elders at tribal conferences and other ceremonies. Otto found the Ubo language difficult to learn and speak during his younger years, however his greatest challenge was to being able to adapt to the native culture of the Ubo. The young Ubo looked upon Otto as an outsider, he did not look like them, he did not speak like them, nor did Otto act like them. Although Otto's skin was deep brown in color, it was not the dark chocolate brown skin color of the Ubo. Otto's features were more Caucasian, thin nose, thin lips, and with dark wavy hair, Otto resembled a Viking with his Nordic features. Most of the Ubo feared him, his forbearance resembled that of the German plantation owners and his black piercing eyes made one believe he could see directly into their soul. Whenever he spoke to his mother, he spoke in German, during that period it was still the official language of Cameroon. The majority of the Ubo population neither spoke nor understood the German language, for the exception of the commands given by the Germans when they were in power.

Otto gave up hope of ever seeing his father, there had been neither correspondence nor any information as to the fate of his father after his father had been repatriated to Germany.

King Nkuno and the Elders decided Otto needed to further his education as he approached adulthood, preferably a career in the diplomatic corps, following in the path of his father. The Council of the Ubo made arrangements to send Otto to Germany and have him enroll at the University of Hamburg. Otto was once again in German surroundings. Even though he had never been to Germany before Otto felt comfortable.

Otto immersed himself in his studies and received high marks and praises from his instructors. Most of Otto's classmates and instructors were aware he had been born and raised in Cameroon but they were amazed at his command of the German language and his mannerisms, as natural as any other German born and raised in Germany. Otto never mentioned his father but the most curious individuals made many inquiries as to his father's identity.

In the meantime, glider clubs were springing up all over Germany attracting many young men to learn to fly. There were rumors that these clubs were the beginning of training for the future fighter pilots of the new German Air Force, the Luftwaffe. The Treaty of Versailles in 1919 had forbidden Germany from rebuilding another military air force but nothing prohibited gliders.

There was a very popular glider club near the university. Otto and his friends decided to join this club, primarily because the girls flocked to the daring young men who were flying these gliders. Tall and thin, with handsome Nordic features and his bronze skin, Otto always found himself in the company of adoring young women.

As Otto became more involved with flying, he became aware that his love of flying meant much more to him than pursuing a career in the diplomatic corps. Otto wrote his mother and King Nkuno that he had made the decision to fly for Germany and put his career in the diplomatic corps on hold. When Otto and his fellow glider classmates approached a recruiter for the Luftwaffe, Otto received the shock of his young life! The recruiter informed Otto that there might be a problem with his application to be accepted but that his glider friends would be very welcome to the Luftwaffe! Otto felt very offended and demanded that he speak to the recruiter's commanding officer. When the commanding officer summoned Otto to his office, he asked Otto the names of his parents and their ethnicity.

Otto stated with gruffness in his voice, "My father is Otto Knoll, a former German diplomatic courier from the German Embassy in Cameroon prior to 1919, and my mother is Princess Tikwana Olagande of the Ubo Nation in Cameroon!"

"Have a seat outside, I will call you back in shortly." The officer responded.

As Otto paced the floor back and forth in the outer office, a senior officer and a man in civilian dress with grey hair entered the command office. A brief conference occurred among the three men. After their discussion, the civilian ordered the two officers from the office and beckoned Otto to enter. He told Otto to be seated, there was a long deathly silence in the room as the grey haired man scrutinized Otto as if he were examining him under a magnifying glass.

Finally, the man spoke, "Otto, why do you wish to fly in the Luftwaffe instead of continuing your studies?"

Otto replied, "I love flying and I wish to fly for Germany."

The man leaned over the desk and stared closely into Otto's eyes. He then spoke in the language of the Ubo and said, "You have grown to be a man Germany can be proud of. If your decision is to fly for Germany, then so be it. Your application will be approved, be the best pilot Germany can produce!"

Startled, Otto leaped to his feet and exclaimed, "Who

are you? Who are you?" The man stated, "That is unimportant, I knew your father when we were assigned together at the German Embassy in Cameroon during the Great War. When we returned to Germany at the close of 1918, he lamented how he would not be with your mother when you were born. Your father had often talked about the son he had never seen and the wife he had to leave behind before he died of pneumonia in 1920."

Without saying anything further, the man hurriedly left the office, suddenly he stopped, turned around and reentered the office. He approached Otto and said, "Otto I have been following your life's progress ever since you entered Germany and enrolled at the University of Hamburg. I had wondered what path you would take now that you have become a man!"

He extended his hand and gave Otto a robust handshake, and without any further conversation, the man left the office. He quickly jumped into a waiting car and sped away.

Otto stood there transfixed, speechless, and oblivious to the two Luftwaffe officers as they entered the office. When Otto regained his composure, he asked the officers the identity of the man who had just left the office.

The senior officer stated, "He is an officer from German Intelligence, we are not allowed to reveal his identity. You may leave now, you will receive your orders to report to flight training school very soon, make Germany proud of you."

When King Nkuno and Otto's mother received the news of Otto's acceptance into the Luftwaffe, they were surprised but resigned to the fact that this was Otto's

decision. Otto's mother asked the King for something to protect Otto from harm if he ever had to go into combat. King Nkuno summoned the High Priest and made the request for an amulet to protect Otto from all harm whenever he engaged in combat.

The High Priest assured the King that it would be done. The High Priest then retreated into the hills with one of the Elders, together they carved a warrior from the ivory tusk of a bull elephant, endlessly chanting the prayers of ancient battles and heroic warriors. The little warrior doll was then dipped into the blood of a male lion then rotated over a fire until it turned black as ebony. After cooling the warrior doll it was burnished with a cloth weaved from hair from the mane of a lion, this was done continuously until it glossed like a black mirror. Princess Tikwana sent the warrior doll to Otto telling him to wear it at all times and he would be protected from all harm. Otto fashioned a thong to hold the warrior doll to his belt to ensure he would never be without it.

King Nkuno called Princess Tikwana to his quarters. When she arrived, she noticed the sadness in her father's face. He asked her to sit next to him and in a sad tone he said, "Otto wrote this letter to me, he requested that I be the one to tell you. Otto obtained information on the fate of his father. The letter states, 'Otto Knoll died of pneumonia in 1920 after his brief interment following the surrender. This information was given to me by a German Intelligence officer that had served with father at the German Embassy in Cameroon during the Great War.'"

King Nkuno continued, "Now my daughter, there is closure at last."

After a moment of silence, Princess Tikwana sighed,

"Now I can be at peace now that I know my husband is at rest."

Princess Tikwana left the room and returned to her quarters, she gave instructions to her servants that she would receive no visitors for the rest of the day and that she was not to be disturbed until further notice.

Meanwhile back at the University of Hamburg, there were joyous celebrations as Otto and his classmates were about to be inducted into the Luftwaffe. Otto hurriedly packed his belongings and embarked on his new adventure, what a happy time this was for Otto!

Charles Toulon was born July 1920 in the town of Saarbrucken, Germany, the son of François Toulon and Greta Steinitz. François Toulon was a native of Tanzania, Africa. François had joined the French Foreign Legion as a teenager and with the declaration of war in 1914 François was inducted into the French Army. After Germany's surrender in 1918, his regiment occupied German territory that included the town of Saarbrucken. François stayed in Saarbrucken after his discharge from the army and opened a small café. François met Greta Steinitz, an innkeeper, and began a courtship that ultimately led to their marriage. The café became popular with the veterans returning home from the war as well as the local residents who found the café to be a good place to eat and socialize. One day François happily announced to his patrons that he was about to become a father, soon François and Greta were blessed with a son, Charles.

Charles grew from an infant to school age in the confines of the café, his mother worked side by side with his father assisting in the operation of the café. Charles helped in the kitchen, often assisting his mother in the preparation of meals for the customers. Charles soon learned to cook and bake, mainly preparing the rolls and pastries. During his early school years Charles became very popular, he would bring his fresh baked cookies to school and give them to the schoolchildren and, very often, he would bring enough for the schoolteachers to get their share. Charles soon earned the nickname, 'the gingerbread boy', partly because of his cookies and partly because of his olive brown complexion. The girls loved to run their fingers through his black curly hair and marvel at his large brown eyes.

When the school day was finished Charles would take his homework to the café, when he completed his homework Charles resumed his chores, Charles did not have the luxury of playing games after school like the other schoolchildren. Charles entertained himself by listening to the tales being told by the veterans of their exploits during the war and imagining himself fighting side by side with them. Whenever a former fighter pilot entered the café Charles would be sure to get close enough to hear whatever stories he had to tell, pilot war stories were his favorites. Charles would daydream of himself soaring through the air like a bird of prey closing in on his adversary and after a fierce struggle emerge victorious as his adversary plunged to the earth in flames!

As Charles grew older and his culinary skills increased, he assumed the role of the main cook at the café, relieving his mother of that chore. Charles' teachers suggested to his parents that when Charles completed his primary schooling that he enroll in a good cooking school to further develop his talents. After Charles' graduation from the primary school, François and Greta arranged to have Charles travel to Lyon, France, and enroll in one of their fine cooking schools. Charles was the youngest student in his classes but he became a favorite among his instructors because of his uncanny creativeness, he would take old recipes and prepare new dishes to the delight of instructors and fellow students alike. Charles also excelled in his baking of pastries, in addition to their delicate texture and wonderful taste Charles would add his artwork to make them beautiful in appearance. At the successful conclusion of his courses, Charles received his certificate as 'Master Chef', which would entitle him serve as a First Chef in any of the fine restaurants in France. Charles returned home and resumed his duties as the main cook in the café. One day approached that would be a turning point in Charles' life. A group of senior Luftwaffe officers from the airdrome near the city of Köln, Germany, arrived at the café for a quick lunch. François presented them with the menu. One of the officers asked if the cook knew how to prepare any French dishes and François replied, "But of course, mein Herr, my son, the chef, can prepare anything you wish to order."

The officer then ordered an ancient dish that consisted of beef that was a favorite among the Norman soldiers in the 11th century, he stated he did not know the name of the dish but he wanted to see if the chef might know. The other officers laughed at such a ridiculous request and told him to stick to the menu. The officer insisted, he looked at François and said, "Does your son know how to prepare such a dish, you told us he could prepare anything!"

François replied, "I will give my son your order."

François retreated to the kitchen and told Charles about the impossible request given by one of the officers. Charles told his father, "Relax my father, during our exams we were often given such 'impossible' dishes to prepare. I happen to know the fare of the Norman soldiers from the 11th century! Tell your customers their dishes shall be ready shortly."

After the officers consumed their lunch, they stated they were very pleased and told François to give their compliments to his fantastic chef. The officer who had ordered the 'impossible' dish told François to have his son come out from the kitchen, he wished to meet him personally. François readily complied and Charles came forward. The officer introduced himself, "Young man, I am General Karl von Kliestermann, Commander of Luftflotte Central, I gave you what I thought was an impossible task but you answered my challenge and emerged victorious! I commend you."

Charles thanked the General and added, "Sir, I am honored that I had to prepare for such illustrious guests, my parents and I hope all of you will return soon."

The entourage then climbed in their cars and departed.

Returning to their headquarters, the topic of conversation was about the Commanding General and his ordering the 'impossible' dish. General von Kliestermann was not in a good mood after being made the butt of a joke. He ordered one of his junior officers to get information on the café, the owner and his family, and submit the report directly to him and with haste.

When the Commanding General read the report, he was both astonished and amazed. The report emphasized that the café was owned and operated by a former French soldier, who was of African descent, and his wife, a German former innkeeper. Their son, Charles, was their principal chef, recently educated in Lyon, France, at one of the finest cooking schools in France. The General had his staff officer summon Charles and have Charles report directly to him as soon as he arrived. Charles was escorted to the General's office upon arrival.

The General asked Charles, "Now that you are home do you intend to bury yourself in the café or are you full of adventure and willing to expand your talents?"

Charles replied, "That depends on any future offers I may receive."

"Well...", the General said, "How would you like to be the primary chef here at headquarters, the rewards are many, not just for you but for your family too. The café could be expanded to accommodate the military personnel that would dine there during their leaves and furloughs."

Charles thought for a moment, "I am willing to accept your offer only if I was the chief primary chef and that I had something to wear to designate that I commanded the kitchen!"

The General called one of his junior staff officers into the office and put the question to him, "How can we hire this man to be our principle chef and designate him with some type of uniform so that all the kitchen personnel would know he was in command of the kitchen?"

The officer suggested, "Let him wear the military uniform of a Luftwaffe officer, but without the rank insignia."

Charles interrupted, "No Sir, without rank insignia the uniform would mean nothing!"

The General said, "That idea is absurd, he would have to be military personnel before he could wear any uniform of the German military!"

The junior officer then stated, "Swear him into the military and send him through preliminary military training. After he completes his military training we can request that he be assigned to our headquarters."

The General put the idea to Charles, "Well young man, what do you say?"

Charles replied, "I agree!"

Charles went through the same rigorous military training as that of any soldier, after the completion of his basic training he received his orders to report to the headquarters at Luftflotte Central, with the rank of Luftwaffe Unteroffizier, the Chief Chef.

Charles was elated, he was one of the Luftwaffe personnel, even though his rank was only the equivalent of a sergeant. The kitchen personnel, the assistant cooks, and the waiters were of many different nationalities and ethnic backgrounds serving the German officers, they had no problem with Charles being their commander. Charles introduced himself to his staff and explained what he expected of them, after a brief speech, he posted their assignments and dismissed them.

All went well for the first few months, the officer's dining room became the envy of the other Luftwaffe bases in the area, Charles received high praises from the Commanding General and his officers for his dishes and their preparation.

Many days Charles could be observed watching the

planes flying overhead, daydreaming of being a pilot in one of them. It was painfully obvious that he never saw a pilot with bronze skin flying any of the aircraft, Charles was also aware of the racial policies of Germany, that for him such dreams of becoming a Luftwaffe pilot were almost certainly impossible. However, that did not deter Charles from believing that perhaps, one day, he could break through the racial barrier and become a Luftwaffe fighter pilot!

The growth rate of the Luftwaffe was not progressing fast enough according to the projected plans of Luftwaffe High Command. There was in-fighting and finger pointing as blame was being thrown back and forth among the Luftwaffe Generals. These grumblings filtered down through the ranks and even the highest ranking officers feared for their careers. The Luftwaffe pilots of the Condor Legion returning from their campaign in the Spanish Civil War were mortified at the state of the condition of the Luftwaffe.

There was a flurry of activity at Luftflotte Central, there was a recruitment campaign running in high gear to get as many qualified personnel, from all branches within the armed services, to transfer to the Luftwaffe. General von Kliestermann was constantly holding meetings with his senior officers to devise ways to meet the goals of Luftwaffe High Command. Very often the General and his staff conducted impromptu meetings in the officer's dining room. Charles would frequently overhear the officers' conversations while performing his duties.

Late one night Charles was awakened from a deep sleep, an idea had suddenly come to him, he exclaimed, "The time has come! The time has come! I WILL BECOME A FIGHTER PILOT!"

The next morning he put his plan into operation, Charles went to the personnel office and obtained an application for flight training. Charles was known and well liked around headquarters, no one had suspected that Charles had filled out the application and placed it in the stack of other applications, placing it near the top. The applications were processed, Charles' included, and passed on through the chain of command. In the next few days the successful applicants received their orders to report for flight training at the various training facilities throughout Germany. Charles was one of the successful applicants! One of the officers in personnel noticed that Charles' name was listed to report for flight training. Believing it was a mistake and someone had made an error, the officer forwarded Charles' Orders to Report to the General's office. When the General read the orders he had Charles summoned to his office.

When Charles arrived, the General said in a calm tone, "Charles, I see here that you applied for flight training, is this true?"

"Yes Sir, it is true." Charles replied.

The General continued, "Were you not satisfied with your assignment here? You had a splendid career here."

"Yes Sir, I understand that, but Sir, you may not understand my feelings. I am equal to any man, I wish for the same things that you wish for and I do not feel I should be denied any opportunities to attain my goals if I am qualified!"

The General interrupted, "Charles, you may find serious difficulties going through with this, there are those that will throw obstacles in your path to prevent you from becoming a pilot. Here you are respected and well liked, you have a good future here."

"Yes Sir, what you say is true and I understand that. Sir, my life is not worth living if I bow down and not fight for my goals. Ever since I was a boy I dreamed of becoming a pilot, I now have that opportunity, I promise you that I will become one of the finest fighter pilots in the Luftwaffe!"

The General looked at Charles for a moment then said, "I must warn you that if you are kicked out of flight school you will not be permitted to return here in your present position, you will be sent to the infantry as a private!"

Charles said, "Yes Sir, I know that and I am willing to accept the consequences, if it kills me I shall die happy! I shall die a MAN, not a glorified servant!"

A period of silence cast a pall over the office. Finally the General spoke, "Charles, I will approve your request for flight training and truly, I wish you success, make us proud."

"Thank you Sir, I really did enjoy myself while I was assigned here and I am grateful that God has given me this opportunity!"

Charles saluted then left the office to embark on the greatest adventure of his life, entry into flight school. There were many raised eyebrows at flight school when Charles arrived, he had to endure many insults because of his brown skin, Charles was also given the silent treatment imposed on him by his fellow cadets.

Eventually Charles slowly won over most of the cadets and his instructors because he stayed at the top of his class and his uncanny marksmanship was the talk of the air base.

One of his instructors said, "This man is a natural, he will be one of Germany's top aces if we ever have to go to war!"

After completing his training, Charles was given military leave to go home. He went to the café and proudly strutted in his new uniform, the uniform of a Luftwaffe pilot, not the uniform of a chef! His parents were very proud, their son came home an officer. It seemed all of Saarbrucken turned out to welcome Charles home!

Maximillian 'Max' Ule was born August 1920 in Berlin, Germany, the son of Shaka Ule and Olga Heinz.

Shaka Ule was a warrior from the Zulu Nation, Africa. Shaka Ule fought with the British Army during World War I. Olga Heinz served as a nurse in a German field hospital, also during World War I. Shaka and his squad became engaged in a skirmish with German grenadiers and was wounded and taken prisoner. Shaka was taken to a field hospital, the same hospital where Olga was assigned. Some German soldiers saw Shaka and his comrades being taken to the examination stations, they confronted Shaka's guards and ordered them to move out of the way. Olga and the doctors at the station saw this and rushed to the scene, as the soldiers raised their rifles, Olga screamed, "Stop!" and jumped in front of the soldier's guns! The doctors, orderlies, and other nearby nurses also stepped in front of the guns! After a brief standoff that seemed to last for an eternity the German soldiers lowered their guns and moved away. Shaka and his comrades could not believe what they had just witnessed! Germans had stopped other Germans from killing them! After the incident was quelled, Shaka and his comrades had their wounds treated, Nurse Olga was assigned to Shaka during his stay at the hospital.

In a matter of weeks, the war ended and all the prisoners of war were returned to their countries, the field hospitals were dismantled and the hospital personnel were sent home. Shaka Ule returned to England and made a full recovery from his wounds. Olga Heinz returned to her home in Bremerhaven, Germany, and resumed her career as a nurse at one of the local hospitals.

As time elapsed, Shaka would think of the nurse who had saved his life and tended to his wounds. Shaka felt he had to find her, to thank her, if only to see her once more! Shaka traveled to Germany in his quest to find this nurse, since he did not know her name that only made the search more difficult. After countless inquiries and futile leads, Shaka followed one final lead that led him to the local hospital in Bremerhaven where Olga was working! At last, Shaka finally found Olga!

After introducing himself and reminding her of that incident in the field hospital when she saved his life, Shaka told her of his unending quest to find her. Olga introduced herself and related that she was happy that he had found her. This tall muscular man, ebony in color with coal black eyes, his face etched with the tribal scars of a warrior of the Zulu Nation, gently looked into the bright blue eyes and pretty cherub face of this beautiful maiden. Shaka reached out and held Olga's hand, they did not speak for a moment, both knew this relationship would be forever! Shaka and Olga were married and settled in the city of Berlin, Germany.

Shaka obtained a job as a locomotive engineer in the freight yards, Olga transferred to a hospital in Berlin. The happy couple was soon blessed with the arrival of their first born, a son, Maximillian Ule. As Maximillian developed from an infant to school age, everyone referred to him as 'Max'. Max had the facial features of his father that became more defined as he got older, the high cheekbones, the prominent flat nose, the steely blue eyes like his mother's and the wiry blonde hair, similar in color to his mother's straight blonde hair. His skin a light colored brown, compared to cocoa with cream.

When Max started school, the other schoolchildren noticed he looked different from them but as they became better acquainted with him, his looks meant little because of his engaging personality. Max was an inquisitive student, he exhibited a keen interest in mathematics and the physical sciences in his early years. His teachers noticed this and conferred with his parents to encourage Max to develop his knowledge in these subjects. Max became interested in discovering how things worked and onc could find Max tinkering with discarded junk. Max' friends frequently followed him to the junkyards where Max spent a lot of his free time, Max would dig around looking for old discarded automobile engines to rebuild and attempt to make them run. His friends would marvel at him whenever he got one to sputter and run, even if it ran for only a brief period.

Max was also an avid reader, he read history books that told stories of the British battles with his father's ancestors, the Zulu, in the 19th century, especially the Zulu's great victory over the British forces at the battle of Isandiwana in 1879. Max would often talk to his father about his father's life in growing up in Africa. Max had this intense desire to know everything about his heritage.

Max progressed through school at an accelerated pace, he finishing his primary schooling and was readily accepted at one of the more prestigious technical institutes. Max became the favorite among his instructors, always seeking more information. One day Max saw an ad in the newspaper that stated the Junkers Aircraft Company was hiring apprentices to work in their aircraft design department. Max applied and after presenting his school records, his application was accepted. When Max appeared for his interview, the interviewer asked, "Are you Russian or Slovakian?"

Max stated, "No, I am German, I was born here in Berlin." The interviewer paused and took a long look at Max, after a brief silence, he continued with the interview.

Max was soon hired, and with the other apprentices, was given a tour of the plant. Max stopped and stared at one of the models of an airplane the Junkers Company was developing.

Max asked his guide, "What kind of airplane is that?"

The guide stated with pride, "That is our new dive bomber, the 'Sturzkampfflugzeug', we refer to it as 'Number 87'."

Max mused, "It looks like a bird of prey."

The guide said with glee, "That is exactly what it is supposed to be, a fierce bird of prey!"

At the conclusion of the tour, Max and his fellow apprentices were given instructions as to when to begin their employment.

Max was excited when he told his parents he had been accepted as an apprentice designer in the design department of the Junkers Aircraft Company. The next day Max gave the news to his instructors at the technical institute. They bid him 'Auf Wiedersehn' and wished him great success.

Max was given the task of designing a bomb release mechanism for airplane 'Number 87'. The function of the plane was to approach its target in a steep dive, release its bombs at a very low level, and immediately pull out of the dive, escaping the blast after destroying the target with pinpoint accuracy. Max spent many hours developing the release mechanism, when he presented his plans to the engineers, they were amazed he presented his solution so quickly. Other plans were submitted by other designers but Max' design was the most preferred. A working model was built and given exhaustive tests. The decisive test would come when it was fitted to the test plane and flown under battlefield conditions.

The day arrived for Max' device to be fitted to one of the test planes. Max was driven to the testing range by one of the engineers and with great expectation Max waited to see his device work, he knew it would work! Silently, Max repeated over and over, "It HAS to work!" "It HAS to work!"

The test plane was flown at a high altitude over the range, after it circled the target, it peeled off into a steep dive, aiming for the target! The bomb was released at a low altitude and as the plane abruptly pulled up, the bomb exploded in the center of the target! The plane flew off into the distance, unscathed! Max was congratulated and given the title, 'the boy genius', in the design department.

An engineer watching the test exclaimed, "The Sturzkampfflugzeug is a success!"

Another engineer said, with a smirk, "That name is too long and cumbersome, lets abbreviate it to the 'STUKA'!

The name caught on and everyone at Junkers Aircraft Company referred to the plane as the 'STUKA'. History has recorded that this name would be used worldwide to describe this plane. This name remains in use to this very day, these many decades later! Max' reputation rose rapidly in the design department, one of his most successful contributions was a variant supercharger for engines, primarily used for fighter planes.

Max was aware Germany wanted to have this plane ready for the military as soon as possible. Max heard rumors around the plant that war was inevitable, Europe was in the middle of an uneasy peace and the rapid expansion of Germany's military power added a hint of truth to the rumors. Max decided that if war was to come he would enlist in the Luftwaffe. Max approached his project manager and confided in him his plan to join the Luftwaffe. A meeting was scheduled for Max to be interviewed by two recruiting officers from the Luftwaffe, Max approached the manager of the design department and stated that he desired to become a Luftwaffe pilot if war was to come to Germany.

The manager replied, "I will prepare a letter of recommendation for you Max, your contributions to the development of the 'Stuka' more than qualify you for a career in the military. The Project Manager informed Max that he was to be interviewed by two officers from the Luftwaffe, Major Wilhelm Schultz and his adjutant, Lt. Josef Schmidt. The first officer, Lt. Schmidt related, "Max Ule, we have your employment record here at the Junkers Aircraft Company and it has stated all of your accomplishments, in particular your designing a supercharger for aircraft engines. Recently you have given your oath of secrecy for all of your future projects, to protect them even at the cost of your life, is that true?"

"Yes, that is true."

Maj. Shultz then queried, "You wish to fly?"

"Yes Sir!"

Maj. Schultz continued, "Instead of being a test pilot at your young age, you could be of more service to the Fatherland if you were a pilot in the Luftwaffe, fighting for your country! Would you agree?"

"Yes Sir! I agree! I would be honored to serve my country."

Maj. Schultz continued, "Our records indicate that your parents are Shaka Ule, an African Zulu who fought with the British Army against us in the Great War and a former German army nurse, Olga Heinz, which she is presently assigned to one of the hospitals here in Berlin, is that true?"

"Yes Sir, that is true."

"Then you see, Max, that we are caught in a very tenuous position, would you agree?" the Major continued.

"No Sir, my parents are very good German citizens. My father has long ago severed his ties with the British, ever since they refused to recognize the sovereignty of the Greater Zulu Nation in Africa. That was how he and his compatriots were conscripted into the British Army during the Great War. Some Zulus still believe they are at war with the British! My father could not find decent employment in England, which is why he settled here in Germany after he and mother were married."

Maj. Schultz continued, "The Luftwaffe needs pilots

desperately but there are racial policies that may hamper the goals to get qualified personnel based on a person's ethnicity. Max, you are qualified in many areas, you could be an asset, based on your qualifications, but I must decide on whether to follow the doctrine of some of my superiors or consider what is best for my country. Max, would you rather stay here at Junkers as a premier designer or fly for the Luftwaffe? I must tell you that the opportunities for Germans with mixed blood are disappearing more and more every day."

Max replied, "I will better serve my country as a warrior, in the image of my father and my ancestors!"

Maj. Schultz and Lt. Schmidt looked at each other then they both looked at Max, Maj. Schultz then stated, "Welcome to the Luftwaffe, your marching orders will be coming forthwith!"

Max left his office for the last time, his supervisor said, "I did not get to know you, but your reputation preceded you, and we all hate to see you go."

When Max came home, he related to his parents what had occurred earlier and that he was soon to begin flight training in the Luftwaffe.

Max' father said, "I know you will make us proud!" His mother said, "Our hearts go with you, we will pray for you, you will always be with us."

Chapter

II

World War II Begins

A STUKA Ju87D Dive Bomber over Warsaw, Poland
September 1939, the beginning of World War II.

On 1 September 1939 German troops crossed the border into Poland, the long anticipated day of the beginning of war finally arrived. The German armored units and infantry raced through Poland with the Luftwaffe blasting a path for their advance. Britain and France declared war on Germany three days later. The fighter units of the Luftwaffe swept the skies clear of the Polish Air Force, Max and his fellow Stuka pilots rained death and destruction on the Polish forces, decimating whole regiments as they dived on the terrified Polish troops, bombing and strafing them. Max activated the sirens, also known as the "trumpets of Jericho", on his Stuka as he dived on his targets; the pandemonium caused by the shrill sound on the troops below caused the Polish army units to flee in panic.

The Polish capital, Warsaw, was bombed to rubble and soon Poland surrendered to the German forces. Poland also surrendered to the Russian forces that had attacked her on her Eastern Front. The Polish campaign lasted only four weeks. The coordinated attacks with the Luftwaffe supporting armored and infantry units coined the phrase, "Blitzkrieg", or lightning warfare! Meanwhile on the Western Front there was very little fighting between the British and French forces against the Germans. This temporary lull in the fighting would last through the winter and early spring. At the time, the media would refer to this as 'The Phony War'.

Otto's unit flew reconnaissance missions over Holland and Denmark; Hans' unit flew reconnaissance missions over the Maginot Line. Neither pilot engaged in combat during these missions. Hans and his fellow pilots grumbled about the inactivity of air combat, the curse of impetuous youth. Otto, however, was content with the lull in battle.

Otto was flying reconnaissance in late October 1939 when he saw a plane in the distance closing in on him. He recognized the markings of a British plane, a British Hurricane fighter. Otto signaled his wingman indicating he wanted to engage this adversary and turned his plane toward the Hurricane and at full throttle closed for engagement. The maneuver caught the British fighter off guard and he turned and flew back to the Allied lines. Otto broke off the pursuit and returned to his airbase, he could not understand why the RAF pilot did not wish to fight. After returning to his base and reporting the incident, Otto's commanding officer explained that the RAF flyer was also flying reconnaissance and the plane was not armed, the plane had only a large camera. Otto also learned that a fully armed Hurricane had eight 303cal. machine guns and was a very rugged fighter. Otto exhaled a sigh of relief; the fighter he was using for reconnaissance had only two machine guns plus his large camera! There would be many lessons learned, by both sides, during this lull in the battles to come. Some Luftwaffe units allowed brief furloughs at this time.

Max' commanding officer gave him military leave to visit his family in Berlin as winter was approaching. Victory celebrations everywhere in the capital made for a joyous homecoming. As he approached his home his parents, his neighbors, and other well-wishers warmly greeted him.

"Welcome home son, we have prepared many good things for you", exclaimed Max' father; Max' mother held him in her embrace, her tears of joy flowing freely and saying over and over, "You are safe, you are safe, and I am so happy!"

Max was a handsome fellow as he strutted back and forth in his snappy Luftwaffe uniform, his friends and neighbors referred to him as their hero. The festivities went on all through the night until Max asked his mother to allow him to go to his bed and slip into a deep and peaceful sleep.

Max awoke late; his parents were having their strudel and coffee when he appeared at the kitchen.

"Join us my son, we have been waiting for you to awaken", said his father, "your mother and I are so proud of you."

After refreshing himself, Max went outside to stroll and enjoy the sights of his neighborhood. Everywhere he went the people he talked to expressed hope that peace would come now that Germany has attained all its territory and united all Germans into one greater Germany. After three more days of rest and festivities, Max embraced his parents as he prepared to leave and return to his base. "I shall return soon, have more of that good strudel when I return."

Charles Toulon's commanding officer granted him military leave two weeks before Christmas. He traveled to his home in Saarbrucken by train, staring in awe at the winter sights of snow-covered trees, farmhouses, the beautiful fields of winter corn. He could hardly wait to surprise his parents, wearing his crisp Luftwaffe uniform, and loaded with gifts for his parents. When Charles arrived at the station, he hired a taxi to take him to his parents' home. As he approached the house, he could see his mother decorating a Christmas tree in the parlor. His father noticed the taxi pull to the front of the house and went to investigate. Charles exited the taxi, and the taxi driver helped him carry his luggage and packages to the front door.

Charles' father exclaimed, "It is Charles! It is Charles!" Charles' mother ran to the front room and looked out and she exclaimed, "It is Charles!" As Charles entered his home, his parents immediately embraced him. The dogs were barking in delight as their young master had returned home. After a joyful greeting, Charles exhibited himself in his uniform then sat down in his father's favorite chair and said, "Now this is the way to relax." Dinner was hastily prepared and after Charles distributed the gifts to his parents, he devoured his mother's home cooking. After such a long trip, Charles was ready to retire to his old bedroom and sink into a deep sleep.

The next day Charles and his parents attended church. The priest offered thanks for the return of one of its service members for this Christmas celebration. The choir sang Christmas Carols and the sermon extolled the hope of peace to come. Everyone in the parish, including the priest, went to Charles to greet him and let him, and his family, know they were proud of him and that he would bring honor to his country and family. After the services Charles' parents took him to the family café, there the patrons greeted him and wished him well in his career as a Luftwaffe pilot.

Charles was worried about his parents as their home was so close to the French border, even though there was no activity in the region Charles was concerned if that changed what would be their fate. All throughout the area, the homes displayed Christmas decorations, people were joyously singing Christmas Carols, and the children were playing while awaiting the arrival of Christmas Day. For the time being, there is peace, what does the immediate future hold? Charles prayed that this moment would last forever, and so did his parents when they were alone in their thoughts.

Christmas came and the Toulon family celebrated with their friends and neighbors praying and hoping for peace. Charles started packing for his return trip back to his base, his mother wept, as she knew it would be a long time before she would see him again, Germany was still at war. François Toulon drove Charles to the train station and bid him a fond farewell then sadly watched as the train pulled away, tears welling up in his eyes.

Chapter

III

The Battle of France

The Maginot Line was a line of fortifications France erected along its border with Germany before the declaration of war. Hans' squadron flew regular reconnaissance missions along the border as the spring of 1940 approached. Luftwaffe Fighter Command had Charles' squadron transferred from the east to the western front of Germany, under the command of Luftwaffe General Headquarters North. Otto's squadron received additional planes and personnel, the Luftwaffe posted new Orders of Battle. On 10 May 1940, the German forces with their Panzers smashed through the Ardennes Forest along the French border; the Panzers overran the countries of Belgium, Holland, Denmark, and Luxembourg in three days. The Luftwaffe launched the coordinated support for the 'Blitzkrieg' attack against the French and British forces!

Otto's squadron was escorting bombers over Holland when squadrons of Britain's Royal Air Force fighters, which included their new 'Spitfires', attacked them. The Spitfires bristled with eight 303cal. wing mounted machine guns. Otto turned his Me109 into one of the fighters he saw closing in on one of the German bombers and hurled himself at full throttle into the fray. As his adversary appeared in the cross hairs of his sights, he released a burst of machine gun and cannon fire that blew off the Spitfire's wing and sent it plummeting toward the ground. Otto climbed straight up then veered off in a maneuver that placed him diving on the rear echelon of the other fighters in his immediate area. A sustained burst of gunfire sent two Spitfires hurtling toward the ground in flames. Otto was a man possessed as he lined up a Hurricane fighter and raked it with gunfire until it disintegrated before exploding! The melee lasted for more than 20 minutes before the fighting broke off and the bombers proceeded toward their targets. Otto had shot down two more fighters; he scored six 'kills' on his first time in combat, Otto had become an instant Ace!

In another sector, over the French front, Hans and his squadron flew ahead of the attacking Panzers, bombing and strafing the French troops retreating in panic. Three French fighter planes, the Curtis P-40 'Warhawks', armed with six 50 cal. machine guns, raced to the rescue of their troops being slaughtered by the marauding Me109s. Hans and his comrades saw the fighters approaching and climbed skyward to meet the threat. Hans dived on one of the planes and opened fire with his machine guns and cannon, causing the plane to burst into flames and crash to earth. Hans' comrades readily dispatched the other two fighters. Hans' squadron returned to base after the successful completion of their assignment. After briefing at headquarters Hans went to his barracks and proudly described his successful encounter with the French fighter, Hans had drawn first blood. The other pilots in Hans' squadron helped him celebrate his first victory with the other two pilots who had also shot down the other two fighters.

When Otto returned to base, he made his report to the debriefing officer then returned to his barracks. Otto took out his 'warrior doll' and said prayers in the language of his elders as he gave thanks for the victories and his safe return; he said a special prayer of thanks to his mother, he knew she was with him in spirit and protecting him while he was engaged in battle. Otto laid down to rest after the ordeal. A few minutes later an orderly was heard shouting, "Where is Lt. Olagande, the Commanding Officer wants to see him at once!" Another pilot went to Otto's quarters, awakened him, and told him to report to the Wing Commander's office immediately. Otto responded and saluted as he entered the commander's office. The Wing Commanding Officer, Oberstleutnant Karl Thiemann, told Otto to help him clear up some facts. Otto replied, ."Yes sir."

Oberstleutnant Thiemann continued, "The gun camera from your plane was examined and it disclosed scenes where you shot down 6 RAF planes on your first combat mission! The squadron leader of the bombers you escorted has reported he owes his life to you when you saved him and his crew from an attacking Spitfire. Is all this true?"

Otto stated, "Yes sir."

"The ammunition from your cannon was empty and you were almost out of machine gun ammunition, were you aware of that?" Oberstleutnant Thiemann asked.

Otto replied, "No sir, but I guess I was low."

Oberstleutnant Thiemann continued, "In your squadron leader's report he stated he had never seen such flying before and wondered how the plane could be built that well to have withstood all the forces you put on it with your acrobatics!"

Otto related, "My plane is part of me, we are one in the same!"

Oberstleutnant Thiemann told Otto, "You are excused for now but remain available for more debriefing."

Otto saluted then returned to his quarters, there all the other pilots of his squadron, piled into his room, congratulating him on becoming an 'Experte', or Ace, on his first mission. Otto thanked them all and said, "I need some sleep!" After they left his room, Otto fell into a deep sleep.

The next day Otto awoke and discovered he was alone; the squadron had taken off on a mission and did not awaken him. He ran to Oberstleutnant Thiemann's office to apologize for not being available.

Oberstleutnant Thiemann calmed him, "Relax, Lt. Olagande, I gave orders that you were not to be disturbed, we are expecting some important guests very soon and I wanted you to be here when they arrive. Go refresh yourself and have breakfast, I will call for you when they arrive."

A small convoy consisting of three staff cars and four trucks pulled up to the gate of the airbase. Oberstleutnant Thiemann's orders were to have them admitted. The trucks contained the camera crews and their equipment, the cars contained reporters, photographers, and their assistants, from SIGNAL, Germany's wartime picture magazine. In addition, one of the staff cars contained officers from the general staff of Luftwaffe General Headquarters North. Oberstleutnant Thiemann sent an orderly to find Otto and deliver the message to have Otto report to headquarters immediately. Otto arrived and Oberstleutnant Thiemann introduced Otto to the staff officers from general headquarters and the reporters and photographers from SIGNAL magazine. One of the photographers, a blonde girl, exclaimed, "What an Adonis! He's tall with classic Nordic features but with that bronze skin color, and those deep dark eyes, what a gorgeous man!" One of the staff officers whispered to Oberstleutnant Thiemann, "What kind of German is he? I have never seen a German so dark unless they had a bad case of sunburn." Oberstleutnant Thiemann said, "Enough of this, everyone is here to meet one of Germany's new heroes, this is the pilot who shot 6 RAF fighters from the sky yesterday, and on his first mission!" Otto had many pictures taken and the interviews seemed endless but Otto was equal to the task as he basked in the instant glory of the moment. Before the SIGNAL magazine crew departed, Otto arranged to have a rendezvous with the pretty blonde photographer.

Oberstleutnant Thiemann told Otto, "Relax for today, tomorrow we attack relentlessly until this war is won!" Otto replied, "Yes sir!" Otto went to the hangar to inspect his 'mount'. The mechanic showed Otto the bullet holes in his plane and how lucky he was none of them hit him. Otto looked in amazement, as he discreetly caressed his 'warrior doll'.

Soon Otto's squadron returned, after debriefing, the pilots told stories of the rapid advance of the Panzers and the air battles in which the Luftwaffe swept the skies of the French and British planes. Otto sighed as he wished he could have been there.

The next day Oberstleutnant Thiemann ordered Otto's squadron to escort bombers on their way to destroy the port city of Antwerp, Belgium, the hub of transport and supplies for the British and French forces. The bombing raid left the city engulfed in flames, destruction and chaos was widespread, the planes then returned to base, no victories for Otto this day.

The campaign in France was to last until June 1940; the German forces raced across France and trapped the British and French forces at the French port city of Dunkerque (also known as Dunkirk).

The Luftwaffe attacked the trapped forces at Dunkirk relentlessly, bombing and strafing the troops in, around the city, and on the beaches. From England came ships, boats, any kind of boat, yachts, naval destroyers, and any other vessels, pressed into service to evacuate as many of the troops as possible for the transportation back to England. Charles Toulon's squadron joined other squadrons, including Hans Thayer's squadron, in the relentless attacks! The RAF sent in all of their available fighters to save the ships and troops from annihilation; Spitfires, Hurricanes, and Warhawks joined the melee with a vengeance! The skies resembled swarms of locusts as the fighters, bombers, and more fighters engaged in the ferocious air battle! Many thousands of dead and dying troops littered the beaches, many ships and boats destroyed, but the rescue pressed on! Charles dived on two RAF fighters that were raking a bomber to shreds; he suddenly turned away, making a loop to face a Hurricane that had been on his tail with its guns blazing! The Hurricane's volley missed Charles but caught another Me109, sending it crashing to earth in flames! Charles attacked the Hurricane head-on and loosed his cannon and machine gun fire until his adversary also crashed to earth in flames! Charles repeated these encounters many more times before leaving the scene then returning, rearmed and refueled, ready to continue the battle.

Hans' squadron attacked the ships as they were desperately loading troops; the carnage was horrific! Hans' squadron was pounced by a squadron of Spitfires; he witnessed the decimation of his squadron as the Spitfires took their toll on the low-flying Me109s! Hans attempted to escape a Spitfire that was on his tail, closing in for the kill! Hans bobbed and weaved like a skilled boxer but it was impossible to shake off this tenacious foe! Hans felt an explosion behind him but his plane was still flying! What had happened? As Hans made a tight turn, he saw the Spitfire that had been on his tail spiral to earth in flames. A Me109 from another squadron shot down the RAF fighter, saving Hans for another day! Hans was to find out later that his savior was Lt. Charles Toulon!

After the last ship left Dunkirk with its precious human cargo, the victorious German troops marched the British and French survivors from the beaches off to prison camps. The news from England heralded the saving of over 300,000 British and French troops during the evacuation! Prime Minister Winston Churchill of Great Britain stated, "The Battle of France is over; the Battle of Britain is about to begin!"

Chapter

IV

A Missed
Propoganda Opportunity

Before being put in circulation SIGNAL's photos and stories had to be proof read and approved by the Minister of Propaganda's Office. One of the staff members read the story of the young fighter pilot who had scored 6 victories over the RAF on his first mission and was well pleased with the story, however when he saw the picture of the pilot he questioned why the pilot was so dark in the photographs. The answer he received was that the Luftwaffe pilot was German of African descent! His father was a former German embassy courier assigned to the Embassy in Cameroon, Africa, before and during World War I and his mother is a princess from the Ubo tribe. Cameroon was one of the German African colonies stripped from Germany after Germany's defeat in World War I. The story and photographs found their way to the office of the Reichminister, Dr. Josef Goebbels. The Reichminister called a conference concerning whether or not to release the story with the attached photographs. The current policy of Germany was to promote pure Aryan racial superiority, not just German ethnic superiority. The proponents of Aryan racial superiority won out and the story with photographs never reached publication. History was to prove Germany lost a tremendous propaganda coup to win over the populations of British, French, and other European colonies whose subjects had suffered at the hands of their colonial masters. Eventually the United States of America seized upon the opportunity to train and place fighter pilots of African descent in the hostile skies over Europe, and with great success!

After the fall of France, Luftwaffe General Headquarters North had Hans' squadron transferred to an airfield near Paris. Hans and his fellow flyers went to Paris whenever possible; they enjoyed the cabarets, the French cuisine, and most of all the pretty mademoiselles. Hans was a handsome figure, medium height, with skin the color of chocolate, dark eyes, and an engaging personality. As Hans promenaded along the Parisian boulevards, he attracted the women wherever he went. One day while in Paris seated at a table in an outdoor café, a high-ranking Luftwaffe officer approached Hans. The officer introduced himself as Hauptmann Adolf Galland, Central Fighter Command Headquarters. Hans came to attention and introduced himself then offered the officer to join him for coffee. Hauptmann Galland accepted and the two engaged in friendly conversation.

Hauptmann Galland sat back in his chair, pulled out a long cigar, and asked, "Do you mind if I smoke?" Hans replied, "No Sir, Herr Hauptmann" and after a brief moment, Hans jumped up excitedly and exclaimed, "Now I recognize you, you are 'Herr Mickey Mouse', one of the great Aces in this sector! I should have known, please forgive me Herr Hauptmann!"

Hauptmann Galland motioned for Hans to sit down, "Relax young man, you are correct, I do have my favorite character, 'Mickey Mouse', painted on the fuselage of my mount. I want the British to know who I am whenever they see me. But I am curious, do you know a Luftwaffe pilot named Lt. Otto Olagande?" Hans replied, "No sir, but I have heard of him, he has scored many victories and is already an 'Experte', or 'Ace'. I heard his acrobatics and marksmanship in the air confound the enemy before they are swept from the sky."

Hauptmann Galland stated, "That is correct, Lt. Olagande is one of a very few Luftwaffe pilots of African descent, such as you, did you know that?" Hans replied, "No sir, I have not met any other pilots of African descent although I am aware there are others."

"You, Lt. Hans Thayer, were saved from an attacking

Spitfire during the final days of the 'Battle of Dunkirk' by a pilot named Lt. Charles Toulon, also a pilot of African descent." Hauptmann Galland began laughing, "Lt. Toulon is also an 'Ace' with at least nine victories at this time!"

Hans responded, "I sent a letter of gratitude to Lt. Toulon's squadron thanking Lt. Toulon for saving my life, I received a nice reply from Lt. Toulon but I did not know he was also of African descent, I will contact him again! I really thank you for this information, Herr Hauptman."

Hauptmann Galland inquired, "How are you doing at this time?"

"At this time my squadron is doing coastal patrol duties, we have little opportunity for engagement with the British. I only have three victories to my credit and that was attained while fighting over Dunkirk."

Hauptmann Galland smiled, "Keep up the good work Hans, the accomplishments of you and your fellow flyers of African Descent are of great interest to Fighter Command." The conversation changed to the lighter moments of the day, such as the pretty mademoiselles that gathered to ogle at these two dashing flyers. Hauptmann Galland excused himself and thanked Hans for the pleasant conversation, Hans came to attention and said, "The pleasure was all mine, Herr Hauptmann."

Hans returned to base, he was exhilarated as he told his commanding officer of the chance meeting he had with Hauptmann Galland of Fighter Command and how they enjoyed having coffee together. Hans' commanding officer exclaimed, "What an honor, Lt. Thayer, you were in the company of one of the great leaders of the Luftwaffe!" When Hans went to his quarters, he shared his experience with his fellow comrades; all agreed the experience was awesome.

Chapter

V

The Battle of Britain

A Supermarine Spitfire attacking German bomber formations over Great Britain, August 1940.

A Spitfire closing contact with Lt. Otto Olagande flying his
Me109E in a dogfight over the Straits of Dover
September 1940.

Other campaigns followed the fall of Poland, the Russo-Finnish War, from November 1939- March 1940, when Russia invaded Finland and claimed northern territory along Lake Ladoga. The Battle for Norway, from April-June 1940, the Germans invaded Norway, beat back, and thwarted the efforts of the British to occupy Norway. During one of the naval battles, Lt. Max Ule dive-bombed and sunk the British Destroyer, HMS Valiant. For this feat, Max received the Iron Cross, 1st Class.

After the fall of France in June 1940, came the next great battle, the Battle of Britain! Air superiority over Great Britain was essential if Germany was to successfully cross the English Channel and invade Great Britain, code-named: 'Operation Sea Lion'. Luftwaffe General Headquarters North moved to the region at Pas de Calais, France. A plan to wage a concerted effort to destroy Britain's RAF fighters and gain air superiority had to precede the invasion.

Britain had a secret weapon in its arsenal, RADAR! The radar towers along the English coast gave advanced warning of air raids by bouncing radio waves off the approaching planes; the radar gave information as to the direction, height, and size of the formations. With this information, squadrons of RAF fighters flew directly to the incoming Luftwaffe bombers and fighters and quickly engaged the threatening attack!

Luftwaffe General Headquarters North assigned Otto's squadron and Hans' squadron to escort the bombers attacking the British airfields along the southern coast of Great Britain. Charles' squadron escorted the bombers attacking along the central coast. Max' Stuka squadron joined other bomber squadrons in the attack on British airfields. The attack began in earnest on 10 August 1940, the Luftwaffe called the day "Adlertag", or Eagle Day!

Otto had painted on the fuselage of his plane a black shield with crossed spears, signifying that he was a 'Black Knight', a warrior from Africa! During the period, prior to the Battle of Britain, Otto had attained 21 victories in the air.

As the air offensive continued against the RAF, Germany did not have the success against the British that it had against the other combatants, losing heavily to the RAF, the Spitfires and Hurricanes took a heavy toll of the Luftwaffe bombers and gave a good accounting of themselves against the fighters.

Returning to his base near Pas de Calais to rearm and refuel, Otto noticed that a badly damaged plane from another squadron had just landed. The pilot appeared unable to get out of his plane; personnel that had gathered at the crash site assisted him deplane and escorted him to the debriefing office. After Otto was refueled and rearmed, he took off and returned to the area of combat. After furious fighting and breaking off contact with the British fighters, Otto and the remnants of his squadron returned to base and went immediately to debriefing. After giving his report, Otto's thoughts turned to the injured pilot he had seen earlier being helped from his crippled plane. He sought out the squadron commander to inquire about the pilot that had landed the damaged Me109. The squadron commander was in his office examining the debriefing reports when Otto entered. He looked up at Otto and said, "The wounded pilot is at the first aid station in the company of the commander, Oberstleutnant Thiemann. That pilot had been escorting bombers when a swarm of Hurricane fighters attacked them, shooting most of the bombers out of the sky and a number of Me109s from his squadron. A bullet grazed his arm wounding him, lucky fellow! His plane was shot up so bad he will be with us until we can give him a replacement."

Otto went to the first aid station to visit the pilot; he was amazed to see the pilot was of a dark hue like himself.

After Otto introduced himself, the wounded pilot struggled to sit up in his bed and stated, "I have heard of you, Lt. Olagande, I am honored to meet you. I must apologize for littering the airfield with my wreckage."

Otto replied, "Please don't be silly, that must have been some scrap you were in, tell me about it if you don't mind."

Hans related, "All of a sudden the British were upon us, they knew where we were even though we had changed our route in approaching their airfields." Hans continued, "I was lucky, I only received this graze wound to my right arm even though my plane was shot to pieces, I shot down two of them however." Otto exclaimed, "The same thing happened to us! We had taken an alternate route and ran into at least 30 Spitfires before we could regroup!" Otto continued, "We were escorting Heinkel 111 bombers, you know how slow they are, and we did everything in our power to save them from the Spitfires, I shot down three 'Spitz' before running out of ammunition! When I returned to the fray, the British broke off and I returned with what was left of my squadron."

The Wing Commander, Oberstleutnant Thiemann, returned to the first aid station, he saw Otto and Hans in lively conversation. Oberstleutnant Thiemann interrupted them and stated, "We believe we have discovered the secret of why the British seem to be everywhere, it is those strange towers they have along their coast! Those towers give them early warning of our approach, we have received new orders for the Stukas to destroy them! Lt. Thayer, you will stay with us for now until we get replacement planes, I have notified your squadron commander and he has given us his approval." Oberstleutnant Thiemann further stated, "I have to report these losses to headquarters, it is not a pretty picture, something will have to be done soon or else! All personnel will stay on the alert." The commander returned to his office. Otto advised Hans to get some rest, Otto then left and retired to his quarters.

Lt. Charles Toulon and his squadron had the task to escort the Stukas in their mission to destroy the towers along the British coast; Lt. Max Ule was one of the Stuka pilots assigned to this mission. On the morning of 15 August, the Luftwaffe launched its attack on the towers. Spitfires and Hurricanes were airborne and ready to engage them. More Me109s scrambled to meet the oncoming threat, Charles' squadron stayed with the bombers. Charles observed two Spitfires speeding toward one of the Stukas; the Stuka plunged into a steep dive followed by the Spitfires. As the three planes neared treetop level, the Stuka pulled up sharply and the rear gunner fired a sustained burst of fire at the nearest plane! The Spitfire immediately caught fire after being hit, the plane then careened toward the ground; the second plane leveled off as the Stuka performed an inverted loop that put it on the tail of the other Spitfire. The Stuka pilot took aim and raked the plane with machine gun fire until it fell to earth in pieces.

Charles exclaimed, "Mein Gott, I have never seen flying like that, that pilot must be a superman! I need to know him!" In the meantime, Charles had his own troubles as a gaggle of Spitfires closed in on him and his wingman. Twisting and turning in tight maneuvers, Charles was able to escape the trap but his wingman was not as lucky, his wingman's Me109 dived to the ground in flames after being riddled with machine gun fire from the Spitfires. Charles' momentary grief of losing his wingman now turned to fury as he flew headlong into the Spitfires, guns blazing as one plane after another fell before the unrelenting fire from his cannon and machine guns! Other pilots, both British and German, witnessed a man possessed as Charles continued to press his attack, forcing his adversaries to withdraw!

Charles discovered he was out of ammunition as the sky cleared of the RAF fighters, he then returned to base. The Stuka pilot that Charles saw shoot down two Spitfires returned to his base and reported the destruction of the towers in his sector by the Stuka squadrons. Charles inquired as to the identity of that Stuka pilot and received information the pilot was Lt. Max Ule. Ironically, Max was also making inquiries about the identity of the fighter pilot that almost single-handedly saved the Stuka squadrons in his sector from destruction by the RAF fighters. These two pilots' exploits reached the headquarters of Luftwaffe General Headquarters North; all squadrons in the area received bulletins that detailed the feats performed by these two pilots, as well as their identities and squadron assignments.

The 'fickle finger of Fate' was drawing the lives of these four African-German aviators closer and closer together. Their individual stories began melding into one story encompassing the four of them.

Before Hans returned to his squadron, he sought out Otto and the wing commander to thank them for their hospitality. When Hans found Otto, he related that Lt. Charles Toulon, mentioned in the bulletin, was the same pilot that had saved his life during the battle of Dunkirk and that he is of African descent.

Otto exclaimed, "Another Black Knight! Hans, I had a black shield with crossed spears painted on my plane, to

let friend and foe alike know I was a 'Black Knight', both you and Charles Toulon have proven worthy to be known as Black Knights, paint your plane so everyone knows who you are!"

Hans replied, "Coming from you Otto, that is indeed a compliment, I heard about you before our meeting here, I once had a chance meeting with Adolf Galland, now General of Fighters, he expressed great admiration of you as one of the leading 'aces' in the Luftwaffe and he also mentioned Lt. Charles Toulon, another ace."

Otto said, "I feel so honored that General Galland had shown interest in me, I don't know what to say."

The two flyers shook hands and Hans departed, Otto watched Hans take off then saluted him as he ascended to the skies above.

Lt. Max Ule read the bulletin that praised him and Lt. Charles Toulon; he sent a letter to Charles' squadron thanking Charles for saving him and his bomber comrades in an unbelievable display of flying and fighting ability. Max received a reply from Charles complimenting him on his ability to handle the Stuka as if it was a small maneuverable fighter plane. The two pilots exchanged letters and the desire to meet one day.

The air war continued throughout the month of August without abatement. One incident would change the course of the air war however; on 25 August, early in the morning, a lone Heinkel 111 bomber strayed off course and loosed its bombs over the heart of London. Although the damage was slight, the British retaliated with a bomb attack on Berlin; again, the damage was slight.

The German High Command became enraged and ordered its bombers to concentrate on a bombing campaign against London and other cities; this became known as 'The London Blitz'. The German High Command eventually cancelled all daylight-bombing missions and postponed the invasion Great Britain, or 'Operation Sea Lion', indefinitely. With the cancellation of the daylight raids against the RAF bases this offered a respite that allowed the RAF to rebuild and expand, the Battle of Britain was over, the campaign was victorious for the British, even though the war with Britain continued!

Luftwaffe General Headquarters North assigned Lt. Charles Toulon and Lt. Hans Thayer to a new fighter squadron together, outfitted with the new Focke-Wulf 190A, 'butcher bird', and the new Me109F fighters. As the two pilots entered the roll call room icy stares from the other pilots met them, one of them approached Hans and Charles.

He demanded in a shrill voice, "Take off those uniforms and stop masquerading as Luftwaffe Officers and return to the kitchen!"

Hans bristled up in anger and shouted, "My name is Hans Thayer, let no man make the mistake of offending me, I am already at war and the war will continue right here where I stand!"

Charles stepped forward and stood alongside of Hans and echoed, "This silly bastard standing in front of us with his crazy demands is standing in Harm's Way! My name is Charles Toulon; let none of you forget it! Touch my uniform or me and...!" The piercing eyes of Charles, aflame with rage, and Hans' muscles in his arms welling up in the sleeves of his tunic as he tightened his fists brought a deathly silence into the room.

At that same moment, the commanding officer entered the room with his adjutant and called everyone to attention. The commander, Hauptmann Günter Ritter, a slim man with a shaved head, his monocle placed firmly in his left eye socket, looked over the assembly of Luftwaffe pilots as they stood silently at attention. Slowly he paced back and forth, then announced in a gruff voice, "This will be the only time I say this, anyone who disrespects other officers in my command will be severely dealt with! We are at war and we will conduct ourselves as soldiers! We will fight the enemy, not each other!" Commander Ritter left the room and retired to his office. The adjutant conducted the roll call then gave the order for the pilots to be dismissed.

Finally meeting face to face, Hans and Charles briefly shared their experiences, including their African heritage Charles suggested, "Let's go to the mess hall and talk over a cup of coffee."

"Splendid idea", Hans replied, "There is so much for us to talk about."

The mess hall was a small abandoned schoolhouse that had been converted into a large kitchen and dining area. After Hans and Charles entered the hall they were approached by one of the other Luftwaffe pilots, a tall blonde youth.

"I am sorry for the way my comrades behaved, I explained to them who both of you were, I had already heard of your exploits. They were shocked to know that you two were Aces who had already distinguished yourselves in battle." The pilot extended his hand and introduced himself, "I am Erich Hartmann, there is enough of the enemy for all of us, like the Commandant said, we will fight the enemy, not each other."

Hans and Charles thanked the young pilot and invited him to join them at their table. Erich respectfully declined and explained he had been summoned to the Commandant's office, "But keep the invitation open for the future." After Erich departed Hans and Charles sat at a table and had one of the orderlies bring them coffee and strudel pastries.

Hans related, "I am glad to be able to thank you in person for saving my life during the battle of Dunkirk."

Charles replied, "I am happy I happened to be in the right place at the right time." Charles continued, "I heard that Lt. Max Ule, a Stuka bomber pilot, was also of African descent. We had exchanged letters but since his transfer to the Balkans campaign, we lost contact with each other. I never got the chance to actually meet him."

Hans related, "I have heard many stories about him, it has been told he handles his Stuka as if it were a fighter, he must be endowed with super strength to handle that beast. The last time I saw Otto he mentioned to me that he had painted a black shield with crossed spears on the side of his mount to let all know he was a Black Knight. He also said both of us, in his opinion, are qualified to be Black Knights. We should paint our mounts with the same distinctive markings so friend and foe alike would know us as Black Knights"

Charles thought for a moment, "That's a wonderful idea, with our brand new planes we should have them painted right away, incidentally, where is Otto now?"

"Word has it he is in the Mediterranean Theatre; his squadron participated in the 'Island of Crete campaign' that was recently captured by our paratroopers."

"I have another idea Hans, to distinguish ourselves from each other we should paint the noses of our planes different colors, what do you think?"

"I agree. I will paint my nose orange."

Charles stated, "And I will paint mine red."

Chapter

VI

Operation Barbarossa

Lts. Charles Toulon (Red Nose) and Hans Thayer (Orange
Nose) flying in their Fw-190A 'Butcher Birds' over Russia,
June 1941, 'Operation Barbarossa'.

As June 1941 approached, Fighter Command had many of its squadrons transferred east to bases along the border separating Russia from Germany and her conquered territory under the cloak of strict secrecy. Lts. Hans Thayer and Charles Toulon joined many other pilots in this transfer; Fighter Command issued orders cancelling all leaves and furloughs, and forbidding any correspondence whatsoever!

The bases in the East were sparse in comparison to the bases in France, Belgium and Holland; they had few amenities, only the basic accommodations. Observing their new base, Hans and Charles resigned themselves to the fact they would share a room together with only bunk beds, shower and toilet. Hans sighed as he thought, "How I miss all those pretty mademoiselles, I wonder what these Polish girls are all about." Hans' thoughts were interrupted when orders came to report to the huge squad room immediately. The entire squadron was assembled and the Officer of the Day called attention. The Commandant, Hauptmann Günter Ritter, ascended to the podium and announced he had a new adjutant, Oberleutnant Otto Olagande, and he stated, "We are gathered here to embark on an historical journey, final orders will be issued very soon, everyone is confined to the base until further orders!" Hauptmann Ritter then returned to his office. Oberlt. Olagande remained to answer questions. Many of the pilots could not understand why they were stationed so far from the fight with England, the Polish campaign was over and Norway had been conquered.

Hans went to Otto and introduced him to Charles. Otto said, "I saw your names on the roster, both of you here make me proud!"

Charles replied, "I am so happy to meet you, Sir, I

have heard so much about you."

Hans added, "I heard about your promotion and I am happy to see you here with us, when you see our planes you will see we took your advice and painted our planes with the black shield and crossed spears. My plane has an orange nose and Charles' has a red nose."

Charles asked, "What color will the nose of your plane be, Herr Oberleutnant?

Otto replied, "I will paint mine bright yellow, like a sunburst; I notice you two are flying the new 'butcher birds', I am still flying the Me109, although an upgraded version with a much larger engine and two additional machine guns.

The final orders came on 21 June 1941; 'Operation Barbarossa' to begin at dawn on 22 June, the invasion of Russia!

The steady drone of the engines of hundreds of planes sounded like the opening first movement of Beethoven's Ninth Symphony! What a sight as the planes took to the sky as if they were flocks of birds migrating to a distant land, a remarkable sight!

Chapter

VII

The Russians Counterattack

The same scenario was taking place with the bombers, the Heinkel 111s, the Dornier 17s, swarms of the Ju87 Stukas, and the attack fighter-bombers, the Me110s.

The opening phase of Operation Barbarossa, throughout the summer and early fall, met with great success for the Luftwaffe and the Wehrmacht, most of the Russian planes were destroyed on the ground, those planes that rose to the air were inferior to the Luftwaffe and were systematically destroyed, the 'Blitzkrieg' seemed unstoppable! Reports all along the front announced the Russians were in full retreat, abandoning their equipment, surrendering in droves, by the thousands! The German Wehrmacht was advancing at great speed, capturing huge areas of territory.

Hauptmann Ritter examined the reports, chronicling great successes, and stated, "Otto I hope this war will be over before winter, I am familiar with the Russian winters, having trained with the Russians here in Russia during the early days of the Luftwaffe. The winters are brutal and have been known to stop an army in its tracks."

Otto replied, "I too hope we can finish as soon as possible, history painted very bleak conditions and eventual catastrophic circumstances for Napoleon's army during his Russian campaign."

Hauptmann Ritter stated, "We must never speak of Napoleon again! We must continue to have a positive attitude about this war and enjoy our successes."

When the squadron returned from reconnaissance, Charles approached Otto and said, "Sir, I have a request, if Lt. Max Ule is with one of the bomber squadrons here in Russia I would like to contact him, we fought together during the Battle of Britain last year."

Otto replied, "I will do my best to locate him. Incidentally, in private you can refer to me as Otto, remember, you are a Black Knight, the Black Knights are the same as brothers!"

Charles went to check on his 'mount', the mechanic pointed to five bullet holes in the fuselage. He told Charles, "You are very lucky; they appear to be holes made by rifles."

Charles explained, "I was flying low, at treetop level."

Charles went to debriefing to await the arrival of Hans; when he saw the bright orange nose of Hans' plane landing he was relieved. After they greeted each other, Hans reported to the debriefing officer. After the debriefing, Hans and Charles went to the mess hall to have coffee.

Hans queried, "Did you notice we can fly for kilometer after kilometer and see nothing but open fields and an occasional dirt road?"

Charles agreed, "Yes, I did notice; no large cities, a few villages, an occasional railroad track leading to 'I don't know where', this is a vast country! I am so glad I am not in the infantry!"

Hans echoed, "Me too! We advance great distances, we swallow huge tracts of land, but there is still more land stretching endlessly, this country is so large that it absorbs you, like a sponge, sometimes I feel as if I am being swallowed by a monster!"

As fall approached, the rainy season began; the heavy rains turned the peasant roads into quagmires, making them impassable; tanks, trucks, and other mechanized equipment became bogged down in the thick mud causing the campaign to slow to a crawl. As Hauptmann Ritter and Otto poured over the reconnaissance reports, they would look at each other and say nothing, both knew what the other was thinking, they both reflected on their conversation about Napoleon!

Winter came early in Russia in 1941; there was a break in the weather as the rain slackened, giving way to freezing temperatures and clear skies. Otto led a reconnaissance mission east, beyond the city of Moscow. Otto observed large clearings of land east of the city, Otto ordered the other reconnaissance planes to go further east and make their observations then report back to headquarters. Returning to headquarters, Otto reported to Hauptmann Ritter.

Otto stated, "Sir, I believe those clearings are for some type of staging area, maybe for troop concentrations."

Hauptmann Ritter remarked, "I respect your observations, you have been very accurate in the past, but troop concentrations, I don't know." Hauptmann Ritter continued, "Their army is practically destroyed, we have confiscated tons of their equipment, they have practically no airplanes to resist us, we are on the verge of capturing Moscow, victory is at hand! We can see the city of Moscow from our most advanced positions!"

Otto reiterated, "I have my deep suspicions Sir, we don't have victory yet!"

Hauptmann Ritter replied, "I bow to your wisdom, I will notify Luftwaffe General Headquarters immediately. However Otto, I hope you are wrong this time."

Winter settled over the front with blowing snow and sub-zero temperatures. Motorized equipment froze, many German troops were not equipped for this severe type of winter, they had to improvise to keep from freezing, many of their horses froze to death, and even their weapons became inoperable in many cases.

The reconnaissance missions continued. Hans and Charles again revisited the area east of Moscow, they were alarmed at what they saw, after taking many photographs, they hurriedly returned to base and told the debriefing officer what they had seen! After notifying Hauptmann Ritter, all members of the squadron reported to the squad room. After the taking of roll call Hauptmann Ritter exclaimed, "The Russians are building up a large army east of Moscow in the clearings we observed east of the city! Convoys of equipment are arriving every minute! We have to destroy them; Notification to Bomber Command as well as Luftwaffe General Headquarters of this situation has put the entire front on immediate alert! Bad weather is moving in fast so be prepared to take off immediately!" Hauptmann Ritter called to Otto to have him come to his office; Otto complied.

"Oberleutnant Otto Olagande, forgive me for my shortsightedness, the Russians read their history and are intent to repeat their victory over Napoleon. I am very fortunate to have a capable officer such as you in my command."

Otto replied, "Thank you Sir, I am satisfied we caught the danger in time, we shall be victorious!"

Every available plane took off. The formation escorted the bombers to the staging areas east of Moscow. The Russian early warning system alerted the Russians of the incoming Luftwaffe; the Russians sent swarms of their new fighters to intercept the oncoming waves of bombers and fighters. The sky was full of what appeared to be swarms of locusts battling each other; Otto led his squadron into the middle of the fray, Hans and Charles saluted each other as they broke away to meet their Russian adversaries head on.

Hans attacked two Russian fighters that were closing in on a bomber, a short burst from Hans' cannon and machine guns ripped the Russians to shreds. Charles was in the middle of six Russian fighters that were circling to entrap him; he maneuvered into a tighter circle and attacked each plane, one by one, until he destroyed all six of them! Otto lined up two Russian fighters that were heading straight for him; before they opened fire, Otto had raked them with cannon and machine gun fire, destroying both of them in one sustained burst of gunfire!

The bombers pressed forward to deliver death and destruction to the concentration of Russian troops below. The Russians had masses of anti-aircraft guns set up around the perimeter of the staging areas; these guns took a terrible toll of the German bombers!

Russian artillery opened up all along the front, their new T-34 tanks suddenly appeared and charged toward the German positions followed by their infantry, clothed in fur uniforms able to withstand the severe cold!

The Luftwaffe was able to save the forward positions of the army from annihilation and enable them to retreat from the Russian onslaught! Hauptmann Ritter's squadron received special attention with honors from Fighter Command for their efforts. As spring approached, the German Wehrmacht was able to halt the Russian advance and stabilize their position along the front.

A serious threat faced the Wehrmacht, the T-34 tank! It had sloped armor, causing shells fired at it to be deflected, extra wide tracks that enabled the tanks to traverse muddy ground as well as icy ground, and a main gun of 76mm that could destroy any tank on the battlefield!

The Luftwaffe came up with one solution; that Ju87 Stukas would be fitted with twin pods of PAK 37mm cannons fitted to their wings. The Russians also developed a plane, specifically armed with two 23mm cannon and two 12.5mm machine guns, to destroy German tanks and other mechanized equipment, the Ilyushin IL-2 ground attack fighter-bomber, commonly known as the 'Shturmovik'! This plane is covered in armor and surrounds the pilot in an armored 'bath tub' to protect him from ground fire. This plane became one of the most feared weapons in the Russian Army's arsenal! Some Me109s replaced their engine mounted 20mm cannon with a 30mm cannon to destroy the Shturmoviks as well as Russian tanks and other mechanized equipment.

After the Russian advance came to a halt, a reassessment of the Russian Air Force disclosed the Russians had introduced high quality fighters to their arsenal. The Russian pilots lacked the training in tactics of the Luftwaffe pilots but they were learning fast. Luftwaffe pilots that had fought in the Battle of Britain had an overall opinion that the Russian pilots did not measure up to the British pilots, at least not at this time.

Hauptmann Ritter ordered the squadron to assemble in the squad room. Hauptmann Ritter announced, "I have received orders from Fighter Command that Oblt. Otto Olagande, Lts. Hans Thayer and Charles Toulon, have officially received the title of 'Black Knights' and each one of them has earned the 'Iron Cross' for bravery in combat! A special ceremony for the presentation is planned for next week pending any unforeseen circumstances." Cheers erupted in the squad room; everyone congratulated Otto, Hans, and Charles for their feats. After the celebrations calmed down, Hauptmann Ritter made another announcement, "Our squadron has more victories than any other squadron in this sector! Keep up the good work! In addition, Lt. Charles Toulon is our leading 'Ace'!" More cheers erupted as everyone congratulated Charles! After dismissing the squadron, Hauptmann Ritter called Otto to his office. Hauptmann Ritter told Otto, "I have that information you were seeking about the location of one of the Stuka pilots, Lt. Max Ule. He is with a bomber group that participated in the attacks on the Russian staging area before their breakthrough that almost annihilated our forward positions. His Stuka squadron is located not too far from here."

Otto thanked Hauptmann Ritter for the information. Otto had an orderly find Lt. Charles Toulon with instructions to report to his office. Charles immediately arrived at Otto's office.

Otto said, "I have good news, here is the information you wanted on the location of Lt. Max Ule, his squadron is not too far from here."

Charles was elated, he replied, "Thank you, now I can finally meet him, I saw Lt. Ule and his rear gunner shoot down two Spitfires with the most daring flying I have ever seen from a Stuka pilot, it was remarkable!" Charles added, "I understand Lt. Max Ule is also like us, he is of African descent!"

Otto exclaimed, "Unbelievable!"

Charles contacted Max, the two of them exchanged information, and the fortunes of war would dictate when they would meet.

Lt. Max Ule's squadron received the new Ju87D Stukas, armed with twin PAK37mm cannon. Max looked at his new 'mount' and whispered, "We will make history!"

Hauptmann Bruno Schneider, Stuka squadron commander, had his pilots report to the squad room for instructions on the role of the squadron in future engagements.

Hauptmann Schneider said, "We have been assigned as tank destroyers, other Stuka squadrons will continue their bombing attacks, we will kill tanks! You received diagrams of Russian tanks with checks indicating the best places for delivering your cannon fire. Dive as close as you can for accurate and deliberate fire. You will find out the T-34's sloped armor will deflect any rounds not placed squarely on target, study these diagrams!"

Max raised his hand, Hauptmann Schneider acknowledged Max, "Let us hear what you have to say, Lt. Ule."

Max related, "I have studied tanks and their most vulnerable weakness is the location of the vents, the engine is right under the vents and the fuel tank is in the immediate vicinity. Shoot the vents and the destruction of the tank will follow!"

Hauptmann Schneider agreed, "Lt. Ule is right, the easiest way to cripple a tank is to destroy its engine!"

The theories and practice were to come sooner than expected, a report of a column of Russian tanks was advancing on a forward German outpost and there were no panzers near enough to save the position! Max' squadron took off and proceeded to the location where the tanks had been spotted. Otto's squadron received orders to take off immediately and provide cover for the Stukas. The leading Stuka pilot shouted over the radio, "There they are, they are coming from the east!" The Stukas peeled off and dived toward the tanks, Otto and his squadron raced to the scene! Russian fighters were closing in also; they had set a trap for the annihilation of the Stukas! Otto screamed through the radio, "Onward! Our comrades are about to be killed!" In the distance, Otto and his squadron could see the Russians attacking the Stukas, within seconds Otto and his squadron engaged the Russians! Hans and Charles flew side by side as a tandem and fired simultaneously at a group of Russian fighters; three exploded, another burst into flames and tumbled to the ground. Otto dived on a Russian that had disabled a Stuka with the 'Taran' attack, the ramming of a plane to disable or destroy it. Otto fired his guns until the Russian plane disintegrated! Other members of Otto's squadron had similar success in repelling the Russian fighters. The remaining Stukas employed Max' theory of shooting at the vents of the tanks and were gratified as the Stukas destroyed every tank! The field of battle was littered with burning hulks that became coffins for their crews! The soldiers at the outpost witnessed an air battle and tank destruction that defied description!

When Max' squadron returned, the stories of the dramatic rescue of the Stukas by Otto's fighters reached Fighter command and Bomber Command. The destruction of the Russian tanks by using the tactics of Lt. Max Ule became the Order of the Day for all Stuka pilots to follow. From now on there would be close cooperation between Stukas and fighters on all future tank destroyer missions.

Max' gun camera disclosed the destruction of four tanks from the 26 tanks destroyed. Hauptmann Schneider sent a note of thanks to Hauptmann Ritter for his quick response for saving his squadron.

Chapter

VIII

The Battle of Stalingard

The German High Command planned an offensive against the city of Stalingrad in the summer of 1942 in conjunction with their attack into the Crimea, to secure the oil fields to supply their war machine. The panzers included in their arsenal the new 'Tiger' tank, armed with the most powerful tank gun of the war, the 88mm cannon, able to destroy any other tank from long distances, often out of range of the other tank cannons. The offensive began with an artillery barrage that blasted the Russian forward positions. The panzers charged forward, crushing all Russian resistance before them. The Russian Air Force pressed into service their 'Shturmoviks' to blunt the advance of the panzers. The Shturmoviks devised a maneuver called 'the Circle of Death', in which as many as eight planes abreast would approach a group of tanks then circle the tanks, picking them off one by one. The Shturmoviks enjoyed much success with that maneuver in destroying the panzers. The Russians also committed swarms of T-34 tanks to the battle.

Luftwaffe Bomber Command committed its Southern Group to the offensive. The Stukas, which employed the 'tank killers' squadrons that included Max' squadron, were also part of the Southern Bomber Group. Fighter Command had Fighter Group South deployed to the region, this Group had fighter squadrons that included the Black Knights' squadron. As the battle raged, under the umbrella cover of fighter planes, Max and his fellow Stuka pilots dived on the Russian tanks with impunity. Over the roar of the battle one could hear the loud basso staccato of Max' cannons as he dived on the T-34s, blasting them into flaming hulks, then raking the fields with machine gun fire as the Russian infantry scrambled for cover!

The sky overhead was its own killing field as Otto, Hans, and Charles, along with their comrades, attacked the

Shturmoviks, sending them flaming to the earth below! The Russians committed hundreds of their new fighters, the Yak-9s, MiG-3s, Lavochkin-5s, and pilots, with much improved skills, to the fray! The air battle rivaled any prior battle the Luftwaffe had been in, including the Battle of Britain! The bombers: Heinkels, Dorniers, and Me110s bombed the city of Stalingrad into a pile of rubble; then followed with incendiary bombs that turned the city into a blazing inferno! To the Russian and German ground troops fighting in the city Stalingrad, there was a greeting shared by all, "Welcome to Hell!"

The Russian fighters, by sheer numerical superiority, overwhelmed the bomber formations and their protecting fighter cover, shooting down several of them. The fighting was so intense the opposing fighters stayed engaged until they had no more ammunition! Some of the Russian pilots used the 'Taran' attack against the bombers, using the propellers of their planes to cut off the rudders of the bombers, sending them hurtling to earth, others rammed the bombers, causing both planes to be destroyed! Surviving witnesses to this carnage and destruction could only say, "I have survived The Armageddon!"

As winter approached, the fighting in Stalingrad bogged down to intense street fighting, house to house, room to room, hand to hand combat! Vast hordes of Russian troops and equipment, secretly drawn from the other fronts, advanced to the east of the Volga River across from Stalingrad.

Opening salvos from concealed Russian artillery signaled the beginning of the attack that eventually encircled the German troops fighting in Stalingrad. The weather turned bitter cold and supplies, food, and ammunition were running out for the beleaguered troops!

The Luftwaffe attempted an airlift to the troops, but the amount of relief supplies able to reach the troops was woefully insufficient. The swarms of Russian fighters sent into the battle overwhelmed the transport planes and their fighter escort!

When Otto's squadron returned to base to rearm and refuel, Otto exclaimed, "Where are these Russians coming from? I shoot down three or four and eight or more take their place!" Other Luftwaffe pilots expressed the same thought; the Russians seemed to multiply like ants, no matter how great their losses!

The German garrison surrendered 3 February 1943. Luftwaffe Fighter Command realized the Russians were forcing a war of attrition upon them. The call for reinforcements from Fighter Command West caused alarm throughout the Luftwaffe; Fighter Command West had serious problems keeping up fighter strength fending off the bombers from Great Britain and the United States of America that were laying waste to German cities!

Chapter

IX

The Battle of Kursk

The Soviet Union Ilyushin Il-2 'Shturmovik' ground attack fighter-bomber, known as the 'Russian Tank Killer'.

After the fall of Stalingrad, the Russian Army slowed further advance to the west to rearm and regroup in a salient west of the city of Kursk. The German High Command saw the opportunity to cut off this large army and destroy it in one great offensive. The Wehrmacht received fresh troops, the newest tanks, and new equipment. The Luftwaffe received the reinforcements it so badly needed. This planned offensive had the code name: 'Operation Citadel'. The original scheduled date to begin the offensive was in May 1943 but many postponements moved the date to the first week in July 1943. The Russians became aware of the coming offensive and made extensive plans of their own to thwart it. Even though bright minds within the German High Command warned against the offensive, now that the Russians were preparing for it, they were overruled!

The battle began with an opening salvo from Russian artillery followed by the response of German artillery, a crescendo of fire that echoed to the heavens! The skies were ablaze as the greatest air and tank battle the world would ever witness began with a fury unmatched in any battle in history! Over 2,000,000 troops, 7000 planes of all descriptions, and 5000 tanks and untold thousands of artillery cannons and mortars from Russia were committed to the battle versus 1,500,000 troops, 5000 planes, and 3500 tanks and thousands of artillery cannons and mortars from an equally committed Germany!

The air offensive began as Me110 attack fighters swept in low over the battlefront followed by the Stukas. The trenches the Russian troops dug for their cover came under sustained fire from the machine guns and cannons of the Me110s as they swept the trenches from one end to the other! The Stukas dive-bombed the pillboxes that housed some of the artillery and observation positions!

The Russian Shturmoviks attacked the panzers! Luftwaffe fighters attacked the Shturmoviks and the Russian fighters sent to give the Shturmoviks cover! A Russian fighter saw the bright orange nose of Hans' Focke-Wulf 190A 'butcher bird' diving on a Shturmovik that had lined up two 'Tiger' tanks for the kill! The Russian fighter turned tightly to bring his guns to bear on Hans; however, the Russian became the victim of another 'butcher bird', this one with a red nose, flown by Lt. Charles Toulon, whose cannon and guns shredded the Russian to pieces! Another Shturmovik fired his cannon at the two 'Tiger' tanks, causing both tanks to burst into flames, Hans dived on the Russian and opened fire at the same time the Russian was firing on the tanks. The Russian careened toward the earth in flames, Hans was close enough to see the Russian turn around in his flaming cockpit and look straight into Hans' eyes while laughing hysterically! Otto joined two Me110s that were strafing Russian infantry. Otto saw five Russian fighters dive to treetop level to intercept the Me110s. Otto slowed his speed enough to allow the Russians to overshoot him, and then he opened fire with his cannon and machine guns as they passed in front of him, two of the Russians exploded, but the other three hurriedly climbed away from the Me110s to escape the withering fire from Otto's guns! Above the noise of battle, one could not escape the deep staccato roar of cannon fire from the Stuka flown by Lt. Max Ule and his fellow 'tank-killing Stukas'. Max attacked a line of T-34 tanks that were attempting to break through a German position at a bridge crossing, the lead tank became a victim to Max' cannons and was transformed into a flaming mass of steel that blocked the path of the other tanks, making them easy prey for Max' guns. Max dived and dived again as he systematically destroyed the other tanks, one after another. As Max was pulling up from his last dive, he saw a Russian fighter bearing down on him, approaching him from the front, Max opened fire with his cannons and the Russian plane disintegrated before his eyes, leaving no trace! Max rejoined his squadron and returned to base to rearm and refuel. The squadron commander, Hauptmann Bruno Schneider, greeted Max after he concluded his report with the debriefing officer.

"Max", he said, "Your gun camera shows you have just destroyed 12 tanks and one fighter plane, you are becoming a one-man army. Speaking on behalf of the squadron, we are all proud of you."

"Thank you; I don't know what to say." Max replied as he wiped the grease and grime from his face.

Hauptmann Schneider continued, "I want you to rest for now, I will send the reserve pilots back into the battle. I will need you and your squadron to blunt an expected Russian crossing of the Volga River to the north of Stalingrad."

Meanwhile the fighter squadrons were also returning to rearm and refuel. Hauptmann Ritter called Otto to his office after Otto finished his report.

Hauptmann Ritter said, "This may sound funny but other pilots that have been in battle with Lt. Charles Toulon told me he 'has eyes in the back of his head', he seems to have an uncanny sense of an attacking plane bearing on him and he is able to bring his mount around and dispatch his attacker. His gun camera disclosed he uses very short bursts to eliminate his adversaries; his aim is superb. What have you observed about Lt. Toulon's technique?"

Otto replied, "Lt. Toulon is exceptional, that is why he is one of the leading aces in the Luftwaffe, it is projected that he will score 100 victories within a month at the rate he is going." Hauptmann Ritter continued, "You and Lt. Thayer are not that far behind, both of you have attained more than 50 kills each. By the way, the Stuka pilot you inquired about, Lt. Max Ule, he is also exceptional. He is responsible for the tactics used by the reconverted Stukas with those large cannons, for their high kill rate of Russian tanks. His record also shows he sank a British destroyer during the Norwegian campaign, he shot down at least two fighter planes and one probable, and he has destroyed at least 30 tanks before this battle started and who knows how many he has destroyed since."

Otto said, "I would like to meet him, as you know we have collaborated with Bomber Command to fly cover for the Stukas when they go on a tank killing mission. He could direct us in the best way to protect them from being pounced when they go into their dives."

Hauptmann Ritter replied, "I was already thinking of sending you over to his squadron to coordinate our efforts to protect the Stukas. I will clear with Hauptmann Schneider, their squadron commander."

Otto found Hans and Charles and told them, "I am going over to the Stuka squadron and confer with Hauptmann Schneider and Lt. Max Ule on how to better protect them when they go on their tank killing missions. I just found out that Lt. Ule sank a British destroyer during the Norwegian campaign in addition to his other accomplishments."

Hans and Charles said, "We wish we could go with you, we would like to meet Lt. Ule also."

Otto replied, "Next time we will all go."

Otto climbed in his mount and took off, heading toward the Stukas. Capt. Schneider greeted Otto when he landed and took him to his office.

Hauptmann Schneider said, "I am glad to meet you, Oberleutnant Olagande. Time and time again your squadron saved my squadron from annihilation from those pesky Russians."

Otto responded, "It is always a pleasure to save a comrade."

Hauptmann Schneider sent for Lt. Ule. When Lt. Ule arrived, Otto and Max stared at each other for a moment before uttering a word. Otto looking into the steely blue eyes of this brown skin man who had the reputation of being a fierce 'tank killer', and Max, staring at this man of dark hue with dark wavy hair with Caucasian features, thin straight nose and thin lips, one of the highest scoring Aces in the Luftwaffe.

Otto extended his hand and said, "I am Oberleutnant Otto Olagande, I am very pleased to meet you, I have heard much about you."

Max replied, "The pleasure is all mine, Herr Oberleutnant, how can I be of assistance? Hauptmann Schneider related that you wanted to coordinate better defensive tactics for us Stuka pilots when we are engaged in our role of killing tanks. I noticed your plane when it landed, you have painted a black shield with crossed spears on it and you have a bright yellow nose painted on your mount. Everyone knows the 'Black Knights', on behalf of my comrades, I thank you and the others for saving us time and time again, I hope to meet them soon."

Otto stated, "You will, be assured, my comrades are eager to meet you too." Otto queried, "Just for my pleasure, what have you done lately?"

Max burst into laughter, "Two days ago I destroyed 12 tanks and shot down a MiG-3 fighter, the day before that I destroyed 18 personnel carriers and many trucks carrying supplies in the rear area behind the lines. Together with my squadron, we blunted an attack by 25 T-34 tanks that flanked our 'Tigers'. Russian Yak-9 fighters appeared out of nowhere and shot down half of my squadron! It was terrible! But enough about me, if it was not for my sharp shooting rear gunner, Erik Streicher, I would not be here either, I will introduce you to him."

Otto reiterated, "That is the main purpose of my visit, to ensure the safety of all you Stuka pilots! And I would be pleased to meet your rear gunner."

Otto and Max then retired to an office and discussed measures and countermeasures to thwart the attacks of the Russian fighters. Hauptmann Schneider had food and coffee delivered to the two officers. Hauptmann Schneider arranged for Otto to stay overnight and rest before returning to his squadron.

Otto arose early and walked to the tarmac where his 'mount' was being refueled, Max was already at the tarmac waiting for him.

Max stated, "I wish to tell you my personal background, I am a descendent of the Zulu, my African father fought for the British in the First Great War as a conscript and after the war he returned to Germany and married my mother, I was born in Berlin."

Otto related, "I am a descendant of the Ubo tribe of Cameroon, my father was a diplomatic courier, attached to the German embassy in Cameroon, and my mother is Princess Tikwana Olagande, I was born in the German compound in Cameroon. Max, I would be honored, and my comrades would be honored, to have you join with us, the 'Black Knights'; I wish to see the black shield with crossed spears painted on your plane as soon as possible, I will send the request for official recognition to Luftwaffe Command Headquarters. You have more than earned the right to be a Black Knight."

Max replied, "I am so overwhelmed, becoming one of the Black Knights is one of the greatest honors I could ever achieve, I thank you, Herr Oberleutnant, I thank you."

Max saluted Otto as Otto got into his mount and took off. Otto looked back and returned the salute.

Otto arrived at his squadron and made his report to Hauptmann Ritter, he then asked Hauptmann Ritter to forward his request to Luftwaffe Headquarters to have Lt. Max Ule officially designated a 'Black Knight'. He then sought Hans and Charles to tell them the good news that Max was to become a Black Knight! The joy of the moment was short lived as the sound of the alarm, alerting all planes to take off, abruptly returned Otto to reality; the Russians were coming!

There would be little time for relaxation as the campaign continued; fatigue was setting in, the weather was hot and dry, taxing the strength and stamina of everyone. The initial successes of the Luftwaffe did little to destroy the Russian Air Force, resupplied with more planes and pilots that exceeded their losses, no matter how great the losses! Fighting in the salient, now referred to as the

Kursk Salient, was grinding down to a war of attrition! The Luftwaffe losses necessitated the combining of depleted squadrons with other depleted squadrons to bring them back up to strength.

The combination of Max' Stuka squadron and Otto's fighter squadron with the addition of two squadrons of Me110 ground attack fighters were deployed to destroy a large concentration of Russian cavalry and armored units positioned in a forest near the front. The Luftwaffe took off in the darkness before dawn; they approached the target area at tree top level. The lead planes dropped flares, illuminating the area, catching the Russians by surprise! The Me110s bore in firing their cannon and machine gun fire while performing criss-crossing maneuvers, causing the devastating slaughter of men and horses. There was no escape from this cauldron of death! The Stukas attacked the tanks; the roar of their 37mm cannons was deafening as they turned tanks and trucks into burning, twisted hulks of steel! The Russian response was immediate! Swarms of their newest fighters raced to this scene of total destruction! One Russian pilot described the scene in two words, "Dante's Inferno!"

Otto's squadron maintained a high altitude for the interception of the incoming Russian forces. Otto's squadron attacked what became a much larger concentration of Russian fighters! Otto radioed back to base, "Alarm! Send more fighters, we are being overwhelmed!" More Luftwaffe squadrons scrambled! Some units responded from bases as far away as the area around Moscow! The battle was on; it became the largest air battle of the war!

The ground crews worked around the clock without break as planes came in to be rearmed and refueled. Some planes were shot up so badly they could not return

to the battle. When possible others received hasty repairs and returned to battle, their pilots knowing this would be their last battle!

Eventually the air battle came to a merciful conclusion, the stress on man and machine was beyond comprehension! Pilots landed their planes and collapsed in their cockpits from sheer exhaustion. Other pilots landed wounded; on occasion, there would be the pilot, very severely wounded, who had miraculously landed his plane, then took his last breath, his plane still rolling slower and slower before coming to a complete stop! Both Russians and Germans shared scenes such as these.

Hauptmann Ritter sat exhausted at his desk with Otto seated across from him. Otto had a faraway look, as if staring across a lunar landscape. Both men sat silently.

Hauptmann Ritter broke the silence, "How much of a squadron do we have left?"

Otto said in a whispered voice, "About half, we need replacements immediately! It is almost impossible to keep up any defense; the men resemble dead men walking, they carry out their duties as if they were robots."

Hauptmann Ritter said, "Fighter Command is sending over 25 replacements direct from flight schools, these men have had no combat experience, we will have to pair them with our veterans and hope they can survive long enough to become worth their weight in salt."

There was no answer from Otto. Hauptmann Ritter handed citations sent from Fighter Command to Otto and ordered Otto to assemble the men. Otto complied. The men reported to the squad room. Hauptmann Ritter called the men to attention then read the Order of the Day. "Oberleutnant Olagande will read the names of the

Lt. Max Ule flying his STUKA Ju87G 'Kanonenvogel' attacking a line formation of Russian T-34 tanks during the Battle of Kursk, August 1943.

following pilots and present them with their citations, these men have performed heroically beyond the call of duty, and their actions are finally being recognized throughout all of Fighter Command."

Otto stepped forward and announced, "Lt. Charles Toulon, receiver of the Iron Cross 1st Class for exceptional bravery and valor in the face of an unrelenting enemy, by his actions he alone has claimed over 100 enemy planes destroyed in air combat!" Charles stepped forward and saluted, then received his award.

Otto continued, "Lt. Hans Thayer, receiver of the Iron Cross 1st Class for exceptional bravery and valor in the face of an unrelenting enemy, by his actions he alone he has claimed over 70 enemy planes destroyed in air combat!" Hans stepped forward and saluted, then received his award.

Otto stepped back and Hauptmann Ritter stepped up to the podium.

Hauptmann Ritter announced, "I present the Iron Cross 1st Class to Oberleutnant Olagande for his leadership against overwhelming odds in the face of the enemy, his contributions to Bomber Command in devising plans to protect and save their bombers and aid in the destruction of hundreds of enemy tanks. In addition he has shown exceptional bravery and valor in the face of an unrelenting enemy and has claimed over 90 enemy planes destroyed in air combat!"

Hauptmann Ritter then placed the Iron Crosses around the necks of Oblt. Olagande, Lts. Toulon and Thayer, then saluted them!

Hauptmann Ritter continued, "Gentlemen, The

Iron Cross is the highest honor Germany can bestow on their gallant fighting men, the award is not given lightly, those who have earned it sometimes receive the award posthumously! The lucky ones however, such as our own heroes, are able to stand here, alive, and personally receive their glory! And now, the squadron is dismissed!"

All the men in the squadron cheered their 'Black Knights', Hauptmann Ritter supplied the champagne, congratulations were forthcoming from every one present, and there were congratulations from the Commander of All Fighters, General Adolf Galland, and his staff.

Bomber Command was holding a similar ceremony, honoring the 'tank killing' Stuka squadrons. One of the squadrons, commanded by Hauptmann Bruno Schneider, called his squadron to attention and stated, "I am pleased to announce the promotion of Lt. Max Ule to the rank of Oberleutnant, and I am also pleased to announce that Oberleutnant Ule has been recognized throughout the Luftwaffe as a 'Black Knight', an honor held by only three fighter pilots! In addition, I am proud to award the Iron Cross 1st Class to Oberleutnant Ule, and the Iron Cross, 1st Class to Unteroffizier Erik Streicher, his rear gunner, for exceptional bravery and valor in the face of an unrelenting enemy. Together, as a team, they are also responsible for the sinking of the HMS Valiant, a British destroyer, during the Norwegian campaign. Both Lt. Ule and Unteroffizier Streicher received their first Iron Cross 1st Class for that achievement. Oberleutnant Ule has single handedly destroyed over 200 Russian tanks, consisting primarily of their vaunted T-34s; and he has destroyed five fighter planes in air combat!" Hauptmann Schneider saluted his new Oberleutnant and told Max, "You and your rear gunner, Unteroffizier Erik Streicher, make a two-man army and I am proud to have both of you in my squadron."

Max replied, "I am stunned, I don't know what to say, thank you, thank you, Herr Hauptmann."

Max and Erik received congratulations from all squadron comrades. Bomber Command sent congratulatory messages to Max. Hauptmann Schneider announced that a special communique had just arrived from Hauptmann Ritter's fighter squadron, sending congratulations to Max; the communique bore the signatures of Hauptmann Ritter, Oberleutnant Olagande, Lt. Toulon, and Lt. Thayer.

Max became overcome with emotion, his eyes glistening after reading the communique. Hauptmann Schneider offered Max a snifter of his favorite brandy, Max accepted.

Max had the black shield with crossed spears painted on his mount. His mechanic asked, "What color will you paint the nose?"

Max replied, "Paint it deep blue, like the evening sky above!"

By October 1943, because of the heavy losses in men and materiel sustained in the battle of the Kursk Salient, or 'Operation Citadel', the German Wehrmacht retreated to defensive lines west of Kharkov. The Russians also halted further offensive action, licking their wounds while they rebuilt their forces. All Luftwaffe fighter squadrons moved westward to new bases.

The new replacements arrived at Otto's squadron. These young pilots had received political training, indoctrinated with Nazi teachings, in addition to their flight training. An orderly directed them to the squad room and called them to attention; Hauptmann Ritter was there to greet

them. After introducing himself, he called roll call then sent the orderly to find Oberleutnant Olagande and have him report to the squad room. As Otto entered the squad room, the new pilots gasped; they could not believe their eyes! Hauptmann Ritter introduced Otto to these young pilots then narrowed his eyes menacingly as he looked into the eyes of these men, his furrowed brow holding the monocle in his left eye in a 'death grip'. Hauptmann Ritter said in a lowered voice, "I am aware what that sighing was all about, I will make this statement once, take a very good look at Oberleutnant Olagande, he is my deputy squadron commander. Oberleutnant Olagande is the holder of the Iron Cross, 1st Class, in addition to being one of the Luftwaffe's leading aces; he is your God! Bury any negative feelings you may have. Any negative actions, any derogatory names or sayings will be dealt with severely!" Hauptmann Ritter then raised his voice to a loud crescendo, "DO YOU UNDERSTAND?"

The young pilots shouted, "YES SIR!" Then Hauptmann Ritter retired to his office. Otto looked at these young men still standing at attention. After a long pause, Otto stated, "You men will soon meet Lt. Charles Toulon and Lt. Hans Thayer, they are the same as I am, Germans of African ancestry and they are also decorated veterans. I am going to assign two of you to be the wingman to each of them. Follow their instructions exactly and you will live, disobey and 'Ivan' will kill you. I will also take one of you to be my wingman; I have not decided which one of you will have that honor." Otto continued, "The orderly will march all of you past three planes parked on the tarmac, two Focke-Wulf 190A's and one Messerschmitt 109F. These three planes have black shields with crossed spears painted on their fuselage. They also have different colored noses, mine is bright yellow, Lt. Charles Toulon's nose is red and Lt. Hans Thayer's nose is orange. As you march past these planes, you will salute them, DO YOU HEAR ME?" Otto shouted.

"Yes Sir!" they responded.

The young pilots were marched out of the squad room toward the tarmac, all of them in a state of shock.

Otto called Charles and Hans to his quarters; Otto said, "Gentlemen, we have a slight problem, we received only 18 of the 25 replacements we requested, and they are all little 'Nazis'!" Otto continued, "I told them that two of them would be assigned as a wingman to each of you and one would be assigned to me. I have their dossiers here; help me pick out three of the worst candidates, I will take the worst one of all!"

Charles and Hans began to laugh hysterically; Charles exclaimed, "That sounds like suicide!" Hans added, "This sounds like the end is near, for everything!"

Otto remanded them, "Enough! Calm down! If we do not do this it WILL be the end of everything, us included! These replacements know nothing of combat, we have to teach them, we must make them proficient immediately, and we don't have any time to spare!"

Hans looked at Charles and said, "None of them have over 20 hours of flying time but they all have over 20 hours of political indoctrination, most of them are 'Hitler Youth' that have just gotten a little older. 'Ivan' will love to meet them!"

Charles replied, "Everything must be terrible on the home front, they must be saving the best for the defense of the Fatherland!"

Otto added, "Perhaps, but evidently Fighter Command does not believe the reports that the new Russian pilot of today is vastly superior to the Russian pilot we encountered at the beginning of the Russian campaign. They seem to have lost sight on the new types of modern aircraft the Russians have developed, and the greatly expanded number of aircraft that are filling the Russian skies! The one good thing we have received from Fighter Command is the shipment of new Focke-Wulf 190 'Butcher Birds'."

After thoroughly examining the dossiers, three pilots' names stood out above the others as the worst of the lot. They were Unteroffizier Hugo von Wassel, Unteroffizier Ernst Schiller, and Unteroffizier Rolf Friedland.

Charles said, "It seems Hugo von Wassel is the worst candidate."

Otto agreed, "He will be my wingman, you two can choose between the other two candidates."

Hans groaned, "I will choose Rolf."

Charles said, "And mine is Ernst."

Otto had the orderly summon the three chosen candidates and have them report to the squad room at once. Otto, Charles, and Hans were standing at the podium when the candidates entered the squad room. The orderly yelled, "Attention!" The candidates snapped to attention, their eyes focused forward. The three pilots resembled boys playing soldier in their slightly oversized uniforms. Hugo was short, thin build, brown hair and hazel colored eyes. Rolf was the tallest of the three, thin build, brown hair and brown eyes. Ernst was medium height, stocky build, blonde hair and blue eyes.

"Unteroffizier Rolf Friedland, you will be the wingman assigned to Leutnant Hans Thayer; Unteroffizier Ernst

Schiller, you will be the wingman assigned to Leutnant Charles Toulon; and you will be my wingman, Unteroffizier Hugo von Wassel" barked Otto.

Otto continued, "'Ivan' will not give us the luxury of time for us to thoroughly train you in the combat tactics necessary to defeat him, and stay alive. Each one of you will follow all orders exactly and instantaneously, is that understood?"

"Yes Sir!" they answered in unison.

Otto commanded, "Dismissed, report to your flight leader immediately!"

Charles and Hans introduced themselves to their new wingmen and each went to a different section of the squad room for instructions.

Otto told Hugo, "I will try to keep you alive for one more day; we fly out at dawn tomorrow to meet 'Ivan'. Remember, stay close to my side, and never let me out of your sight! Now, let me go over a few pointers in combat tactics."

Hugo replied, "Yes Sir! You can count on me."

As dawn broke, a grey haze settled over the bleak countryside, the steady drone of engines reminded one of the awakenings of eagles preparing to soar into the heavens in search of prey. A flare shot skyward signaled takeoff; the fighter squadrons took off and raced to a prearranged meeting with Stuka 'tank killer' squadrons, one of the Stuka squadrons led by Oberleutnant Max Ule. Soon the lead observation plane spotted the concentration of Russian tanks and infantry in their staging area, the observer yelled over the radio, "Enemy to the east, ATTACK!"

A gaggle of Stukas peeled off and went into their dive on the unsuspecting tanks and trucks below, their cannons and bombs raining fire and destruction on the staging area, turning the landscape into a vast wasteland of burning twisted steel! The low-flying fighter squadrons followed, strafing the area, destroying targets of opportunity! The squadrons flying at high altitude were on the alert to intercept the incoming Russian fighters; Otto's squadron was one of the interceptor squadrons. A command came over the radio, "Here they come!" As the Russians raced to the scene, Otto radioed Hugo, "Remember to stay close to me!" The main body of Russian fighters chased after the escaping Stukas, Otto flew his plane alongside the pursuing Russian planes. Otto called to Hugo, "Bring your plane to bear on the Russian behind me as I dive into their formation, when you have him in your sights, KILL HIM! " Otto dived into the formation and released withering fire on the nearest plane, sending it hurtling toward the ground in a ball of fire! A Russian got on Otto's tail but Hugo was there, sending a burst of machine gun fire into the Russian, the Russian's plane caught fire and plunged earthward! Hugo shouted into his radio, "I got him! I got him!"

Hans dived behind a formation of six fighters. Hans called to Rolf, "Join me, pull up so we can attack in tandem, hurry!" Rolf pulled his plane up to Hans, wingtip to wingtip. The two planes closed on the formation of Russians, Hans yelled, "Now Rolf, SHOOT! SHOOT!" The two planes fired long bursts of cannon and machine gun fire into the formation, the Russians fell from the sky in flaming balls of debris!

Three Russian fighters peeled off to attack Charles and Ernst, Charles told Ernst, "Dive straight down and do not level off until you can almost touch the grass!" Charles dived then made a sharp turn to his left, he then

Russian 'Shturmoviks' attacking a German mechanized column during the Battle of Kursk, August 1943.

pulled his plane into a steep climb. The Russians were still in their dive when Charles ascended into his climb. Charles rolled over and lined up the Russians catching them from the rear. As the Russians attempted to escape, Ernst was ascending into a steep climb that placed him below the Russians. Charles shouted to Ernst, "KILL THEM!" Charles' guns fired on the Russians as he was closing in, destroying two of them, and Ernst's guns dispatched the other Russian!

The Luftwaffe scored a great victory this day; the fighters were able to protect the Stukas while they carried out their role of the destruction of Russian armor and personnel. Overall, the fighter losses were light, the Russians suffered heavy losses in fighters. The tactics devised by Oberleutnant Otto Olagande and Oberleutnant Max Ule paid off handsomely.

Returning to base Otto was pleased to report to Hauptmann Ritter that the replacement pilots had made a good accounting of themselves, Otto related, "Of the 18 that went aloft, only two did not return. They scored ten kills among them. Charles' wingman, Unteroffizier Ernst Schiller scored one kill; Hans' wingman, Unteroffizier Rolf Friedland scored three kills; and my wingman, Unteroffizier Hugo von Wassel scored one kill."

Hauptmann Ritter exclaimed to the squadron, "Good, very good, today was a good day for the Luftwaffe!"

Hauptmann Ritter later told Otto, "On a lighter note, I received information that your wingman, Hugo von Wassel is the son of General Albert von Wassel, retired from the cavalry, having served in the First Great War. He will be a happy father when he learns his son has scored his first kill."

The "Good days for the Luftwaffe" rhetoric occurred less frequently as time went on. The German Wehrmacht did not fare as well as the Luftwaffe, the overwhelming numerical superiority of Russian tanks, infantry and artillery, steadily ground their way westward! The Shturmoviks appeared in huge numbers over the front, and with their fighter escorts, they overwhelmed the efforts of the Luftwaffe to stop them from their relentless destruction of the panzers!

Chapter

X

Major Sergei Ostrovanov,
Russian Ace of Aces

Major Sergei Ostrovanov, Russian 'Ace of Aces' with 23 con-
firmed air victories over the Luftwaffe flying his Lavochkin
La-7 'Red Death' fighter over the Kharkov Salient
November 1943.

The Russian Air Force Command South became aware of the existence of a fighter squadron that had been operating in the area west of Kharkov that had three Aces sporting a black shield with crossed spears painted on the fuselage of their planes. This squadron was responsible for the continuing destruction of Russian fighters, Shturmoviks, and bombers in alarmingly high numbers. This squadron also produced some of the highest scoring aces along the Eastern Front. In this squadron, the planes were described as one Me109 with a bright yellow nose, two Focke-Wulf 190s, one with a bright orange nose and one with a bright red nose. The Russian Air Force Command issued a bulletin offering a bounty on the heads of the three Luftwaffe Aces sporting the black shield with crossed spears on their mounts. Luftwaffe Headquarters discovered the bulletin and passed the information on to all Luftwaffe fighter squadrons on the Eastern Front. When Otto's squadron received the information of the bounty, laughter resounded throughout the base. When the Black Knights heard about it, Otto, Charles and Hans laughed the loudest! The Russian Air Force issued another bulletin, in part it stated, "Major Sergei Ostrovanov, of the Red Guard Air Division, has challenged the three Luftwaffe Aces that have the black shield with crossed spears painted on their mounts to a duel to the death! Major Ostrovanov will meet each Ace, one at a time, until he has disposed of all three of them!"

When this latest news reached the Black Knights, they laughed harder than ever. Otto gave Hans and Charles a proposition, "Let's draw the highest card from a deck to see who eliminates this Russian." Charles and Hans agreed. This scenario was reminiscent of a duel that took place in the city of Stalingrad the year before, the duel between two top snipers, the Russian, Vassili Zaitsev, the top Russian sniper in Stalingrad, and the

German, Major Konings, director of a sniper school in Berlin. The German High Command had sent Major Konings to Stalingrad specifically to kill Vassili Zaitsev. After many days of stalking each other in the city, the duel finally ended with Vassili Zaitsev shooting Major Konings between the eyes, the Russian the victor.

An orderly produced a deck of cards. Otto, Hans and Charles each drew a card, and the winning card, the King of Spades, was drawn by Otto!

The Luftwaffe issued its bulletin, "Oberleutnant Otto Olagande will be the first pilot to meet Major Ostrovanov in a duel to the death!" The scene of the battle would be in the skies west of Kharkov, the date, 30 November 1943, one week away, hopefully a clear day, at 6:30AM. The only planes in the area during the duel would be those recording the event. There was an ominous lull in the ground battle as the day of the duel approached.

The Luftwaffe obtained information that Major Sergei Ostrovanov was one of Russia's leading aces, having 23 confirmed kills; his mount being one of Russia's most modern fighters, the Lavochkin, La-7, armed with three 20mm cannon, Major Ostrovanov's plane was colored a solid red.

Major Sergei Ostrovanov was born October 1919 in the town of St. Petersburg, the son of Theodore Ostrovanov, a schoolteacher, and his wife Sonja. Sergei studied piano at an early age and became a promising student. As Sergei grew older, he witnessed the change in Russia from the Tsarists to the Communists, the armed clashes in the streets, the bloodshed and the purges. Sergei's parents urged him to take up a military career. Sergei followed their advice and was accepted in the cavalry where he received his commission. Sergei exercised religiously, building up his body to better handle his duties as a cavalry officer. Russia's fledging air force was seeking volunteers and Sergei answered the call. Sergei first entered combat in the skies over Moscow, attacking the Wehrmacht and Luftwaffe during the fall and winter of 1941. Sergei honed his skills well as he entered the fray over Stalingrad, he is reported to have shot down two Luftwaffe fighters and three bombers in one sortie, for this he was awarded his first Hero of the Soviet Union Citation, and since then he has attained a score of 23 confirmed kills.

Otto would fly his newest mount, the Messerschmitt Me109G, armed with four 12.5mm machine guns and a 30mm engine mounted cannon. During the week, Otto's chief mechanic worked over his mount, fine-tuning the engine and checking all systems. Otto cleaned and checked his guns, no detail was overlooked. As the fateful day approached the weather conditions were expected to be perfect, the scheduled sunrise was 6:45AM.

Otto had gone to bed early and arose at 4:00AM to take a hot shower and shave. He put on his dress uniform, draped his Iron Cross, 1st Class, around his neck, and then checked to make sure his tiny warrior doll was securely fastened to his belt. Otto walked to the mess hall to have a cup of coffee. Charles and Hans met him, no words were passed between them, the three of them entered the hall and there was the entire squadron, standing at attention, with a surprise visitor, Oblt. Max Ule. Everyone was silent. Otto motioned for everyone to be seated. Otto drank his coffee, saluted the entire squadron, then walked to the tarmac and donned his flight suit over his uniform. His mechanic had his engine running; Otto climbed into his mount, he grabbed the parachute and threw it to the ground, Otto yelled, "I don't need it!" Everyone cheered as Otto revved up his mount and took off, soaring into the heavens above! Russia's champion, Major Ostrovanov had a similar sendoff from his fellow comrades.

The site of the battle presented the perfect arena, the sky so clear, no clouds, and the bright sunshine. As the combatants approached, they slowed their speed, and then moved very close to each other, they began closely examining and scrutinizing each other. After staring at each other they saluted then veered off, both ascending into the heavens above, to perform their 'Dance of Death'!

The planes carrying the war correspondents, radio announcers, news photographers, and movie crews, recorded in detail this meeting of the combatants.

Chapter

XI

The Duel

Major Sergei Ostrovanov in a Duel to the Death with Oberlt. Otto Olagande over the Kharkov Salient, 30 November 1943.

The Russian leveled off and made a right turn, keeping the curve until he slowly came behind Otto. Otto watched closely, waiting for the precise moment to allow the Russian to attack from the rear. Otto banked his mount into a sudden climbing maneuver, looped into a sharp diving right turn, about to line up the Russian in his sights! The Russian turned sharply left and veered off into a steep dive.

Otto mused, "Great maneuver, no wonder he is one of Russia's finest!"

Otto slowly dived in a great circle pattern, he knew the Russian would level off but he had to be sure where the Russian would be when that maneuver occurred.

Major Ostrovanov whispered to himself, "He is a very patient fellow; he is watching me so closely, waiting for the first mistake, no matter how small."

Otto banked his plane to the right and in a tight loop; he dived on the position he had calculated the Russian would be when the Russian leveled off. Otto let loose a burst of machine gun fire; Major Ostrovanov made a sharp dive, barely escaping the bullets from Otto's guns.

Both planes leveled off at treetop level, the Russian opened full throttle to escape Otto as he closed in on the Russian's tail. The two warriors twisted and turned in tight spirals, Otto pushing his plane to greater speed inching closer and closer to the Russian. The Russian did a full barrel roll and extended the flaps on his wings, putting the brakes on his mount almost causing it to stall. Otto overshot his adversary then went into a steep climb to avoid a collision! Otto said, "Mein Gott, he is really good!" Major Ostrovanov made a wide left turn to meet Otto head-on and then open up with his cannons. Otto had been in this maneuver many times in the past so he expected the eventual burst of Russian cannon fire. At the precise moment, Otto went into a steep dive and the shells whistled by, passing over his head! The Russian also dived, attempting to get on Otto's tail, Otto murmured, "I almost got caught trying to outrun him, not this time!" Otto extended his wing flaps and strained with all his strength to twist his mount into an extremely small tight turn to his left, as the Messerschmitt abruptly slowed, the Russian's red mount zoomed past. Otto opened his engine full throttle, calling on the supercharger to give its all, Otto's hands gripped the controls with all his strength as he quickly performed a tight figure eight loop and came under the Russian's red mount. For a brief microsecond, the Russian lost him; suddenly Major Ostrovanov saw Otto ascending toward him. The Russian attempted twisting maneuvers left then right then left again but to no avail, Otto matched him move for move, rapidly closing. As Major Ostrovanov's red mount filled Otto's windscreen, Otto knew he would not miss. Otto pressed the trigger, his machine guns opened fire, raking the Russian plane until it caught fire and stalled. Otto then flipped the switch on his cannon and fired a short burst, the shells ripped into the Russian plane causing it to explode, leaving little trace of its existence!

Otto performed a victory roll and returned to base. Both the German and Russian news teams had recorded the entire fight sequence. The news of Otto's victory resounded throughout the Eastern Front, cheers from the Germans, and silence from the Russians.

When Otto landed, the entire squadron was there to greet him; they gave him a hero's welcome as he wearily climbed from his plane. Charles, Hans, and Max embraced him before his feet touched the ground. Otto heard a loud voice cry out, "Move out of the way, let me get through!" Otto looked over the crowd and saw Hugo von Wassel, his wingman, running toward him. Otto shouted, "Let him through! Let him through!" Max and Hugo carried Otto on their shoulders to the mess hall.

"Let me report first before celebrating!" Otto said with a laugh.

Hauptmann Günter Ritter and the Wing Commander, Oberstleutnant Kurt Mueller, were there to greet him; Oberstleutnant Mueller shook Otto's hand and saluted him, then in his booming voice, shouted, "Job well done, we are all proud of you, the Luftwaffe is proud of you. I have a communique from Fighter Command, in part it states, 'Congratulations Oberleutnant Otto Olagande on your great victory, Luftwaffe Fighter Command honors you.' signed by the Commanding General of Fighters, Adolf Galland!"

Hauptmann Ritter stepped forward and shook Otto's hand then saluted him. The squadron cheered without letup as they all crowded into the mess hall.

Hauptmann Ritter asked Otto "Is there anything we can do for you at this time?"

Otto replied, "Yes, I would like to get some rest, my strength is drained, my body craves rest."

Otto retired to his quarters, he draped himself across his bed and immediately fell into a deep sleep. Charles and Hugo entered Otto's room and removed his flight suit, his uniform, took the Iron Cross from around his neck, then covered him with a blanket. Charles and Hugo looked at each other in silence as they noticed Otto's 'warrior doll' clutched tightly in his left hand, they decided to leave it there.

Otto awakened later that evening, he dressed then walked to the mess hall where everyone was still celebrating, the cheers rang out as Otto entered. Otto grabbed a bottle of champagne and announced, "Everyone fill his glass and join me in a toast!" They all gathered around Otto as he stated, "I toast my most worthy adversary, Major Sergei Ostrovanov; he was one of the best opponents I have ever faced. For the exception of one small mistake, the roles would be reversed, he was a great warrior!"

Everyone raised their glasses and cheered. The celebration went on until the early hours of the morning. Finally, after everyone became exhausted, they retired.

The Russians also held a special ceremony for their fallen champion, a more somber ceremony. They sent a communique to Luftwaffe Fighter Command acknowledging Oberleutnant Olagande as a gallant and resourceful opponent. When Otto received his copy of the communique, he related he felt humbled after reading it.

Otto said, "What more can be said about a warrior when the enemy recognizes that warrior and describes him in such complimentary terms as gallant and resourceful."

Chapter

XII

The Luftwaffe's Dilemma

The lull in the fighting ceased, the Russians began the year of 1944 with a renewed offensive westward. The Luftwaffe relocated their bases further west. One of the new hastily constructed bases had facilities to accommodate fighters and bombers, Otto's fighter squadron and Max' bomber squadron shared this base.

Returning from a reconnaissance mission, Hans with his wingman, Rolf Friedland, reported the construction of a large Russian airbase in the region of Brest-Litovsk.

The Wing Commander, Oberstleutnant Mueller, called all squadron commanders and their deputies together and announced, "Gentlemen, the Russians are constructing airbases to cover their offensive that appears to be aimed toward Rumania. Our main oil supply comes from those Rumanian oil fields, we will make every effort to stop and destroy their forces. Our intelligence has also warned us there is an imminent attack on our bases by their bomber forces!"

Otto and Hauptmann Ritter conferred on the preparations for such a herculean task, "Our squadron is at 60% strength and counting the other squadrons in our Wing, the Wing is only at 45% strength."

Hauptmann Ritter continued, "We will have to work our mechanics mercilessly without letup to keep our planes airworthy. Otto, you and the other pilots must be prepared to fly sortie after sortie until you drop! Don't be surprised if you see me up there with you!"

Otto replied, "Believe me I do understand! Now I know how those RAF pilots felt during the 'Battle of Britain' when we had them by the throat!"

Oberstleutnant Mueller ordered all bombers aloft,

their mission to destroy the airfields at Brest-Litovsk. Max' squadron of Stukas was included with the Heinkel 111s and the Dornier 17s. The fighter squadrons were already airborne, preceding the bombers on their way to their targets.

Simultaneously, the Russian fighters raced westward, anticipating the challenge to engage the Luftwaffe formations. Following the Russian fighters were the lumbering heavy and medium Russian bombers, with their fighter escort. As Otto was later to observe, "There were so many Russians, from a distance they resembled a grey cloud!"

As the two forces closed for battle, the crowded skies left little room for maneuvers, the threat of collisions was inevitable. Hans and his wingman, Rolf, used the 'tandem' attack, wingtip to wingtip, as they closed. On Hans' signal, Rolf closed on the nearest Russian bomber, a giant 4-engine Petlyakov Pe8, and opened fire, sending the hapless foe flaming earthward! Hans fired several short bursts at the close formation hitting and destroying two Russian La5 fighters that flew across his sights!

Charles and his wingman, Ernst, climbed then rolled over into a shallow dive, the two planes so close they resembled one plane with two fuselages, they accelerating into the enemy formations, guns blazing simultaneously! Their concentrated fire sent another of the giant 4-engine Petlyakov bombers hurtling toward earth.

Otto and his wingman, Hugo, approached from a high altitude then banked their planes into a steep dive with guns blazing; the Russians broke formation and became easy prey for the other Luftwaffe fighters.

The Luftwaffe bomber squadrons arrived at the

Russian air bases and dived on the fuel storage tanks and trucks, bombing and strafing until there were huge fires erupting everywhere, consuming everything.

Instantly, Russian fighters from the famous 'Red Guard Air Division' appeared. With reckless abandon, the Russians chased after the Luftwaffe bombers and ripped into their formations sending many of them flaming to their death! Otto and his wingman, Hugo, watched helplessly as the volume of Russian fighters was so great they kept the Luftwaffe fighters busy while their other fighters decimated the bomber squadrons!

Returning to base to rearm and refuel Otto assessed the losses his squadron suffered; five of the newer replacements were missing in action in addition to two veteran pilots.

Otto mumbled to himself, "The Russians seem to be content to bleed us dry, we destroy so many of them but they replace two for every one they lose! They are slowly killing us, we now have more planes than men to fly them!"

Otto paced back and forth while his plane was being rearmed and refueled. Hugo's plane also landed and was being serviced. Hugo walked over to Otto and put his hand on Otto's shoulder. Otto turned around, looked at Hugo, and said, "Hugo, I will tell you a true parable about life in the jungle. In the jungle when the 'soldier ants' assemble, there are billions and billions of them, each ant has a specific task like any soldier in any army. When the ants begin their trek, the lions, elephants, and all other living creatures, including man, immediately stop whatever they are doing and run for their lives. As the ants march forward, they devour everything in their path. You can trample millions of them, dig trenches and fill them with water to drown them, fill more trenches with burning oil to burn them, nothing stops them, they march over the dead carcasses of other fallen ants, they are relentless! They continue to advance like a sea of molten lava, nothing stops them! The Russians are doing the very same thing to us."

Hugo stared silently at Otto as Otto caressed his warrior doll, after a moment Hugo replied, "I agree with your analogy, the Russians suffer huge losses but continue to march, no matter what! Curse them!"

After a pause, Hugo made a request, "Mein Herr, I wish you would tell me the story of your 'warrior doll', many of the veteran pilots that have flown with you describe its magical powers that have saved you from harm many times in the past."

Otto chuckled then said, "There will be time to tell you that story at another time, perhaps I can find you some more Russians."

Hugo laughed, "There are so many, I see them in my sleep! God help us!"

Otto and Hugo hurriedly gave their report to the debriefing officer then returned to their planes and took off, returning to the battle.

Charles and his wingman, Ernst, landed to rearm and refuel. They ran to Hauptmann Ritter as he was walking to the office of the debriefing officer.

Charles told the commander, "I feel like I left a rainstorm, instead of raindrops, bullets and shells! I thank God these 'Butcher Birds' are built so rugged, mine in particular!"

Ernst added, "There must be 20 or more holes in my plane too! One of my oil lines was hit; I barely made it back here!"

"Ernst you stay here until you get your plane patched up. There will always be more Russians." After being rearmed and refueled, Charles took off and returned to the battle. Hans and Rolf arrived shortly after Charles took off. They reported to Hauptmann Ritter. "Herr Hauptmann, Rolf and I personally accounted for at least 10 'kills', but the sky is still filled with Russian planes!"

Rolf exclaimed, "They seem to multiply, like rabbits!"

Hauptmann Ritter replied, "I appreciate your efforts, you may leave to continue your mission!"

After Hans and Rolf left the commander, Hauptmann Ritter sank in his chair, removed his monocle, and wiped it gently with his handkerchief and in an inaudible tone he cursed and exclaimed, "We needed fleets of long ranged bombers to travel to the Ural Mountains region and destroy the bases where those fresh Russian troops and aviators come from! We are just scratching the surface fighting them here! Why could not our Fuehrer and his High Command see this? We need a miracle or this war is lost!"

Bomber Command knew the serious trouble it was encountering when the remains of their bomber force straggled in. Many planes were total losses when they landed, many had wounded crewmembers, and a few brought home deceased crewmembers.

Max and the few remaining Stukas landed, Hauptmann Schneider was at the field to greet them. Hauptmann

Schneider inquired, "How did it go?"

Max replied, "We knocked out the airbase we were assigned to, we destroyed their fuel depot and other facilities, but as you can see, very few of us survived! I hope the other squadrons did better at destroying the other airbases."

"Go and make your report Max, there will be revisions made on how we use our bomber force in our future raids." Hauptmann Schneider sighed.

Max and Erik reported to the debriefing officer, Max told Erik, "You don't have to be here, I will make the report, get something to eat and get a little rest while you can."

"Thank you Sir." Erik retired to his quarters.

The fighters began returning, many limping in with bullet riddled planes, some pilots wounded, but the majority of those that survived had racked up huge scores of 'kills' from this giant air battle. Hauptmann Ritter was pleased to see his fighters returning with excellent combat reports but he knew Fighter Command could not suffer these losses and remain an effective fighting force. Hauptmann Ritter stood outside his office to check the returning fighters, a smile crept across his face as he observed a red nose plane, then an orange nose plane, and finally a yellow nose plane coming in for a landing. He went back inside his office awaiting the reports of his fighters.

After the debriefing Otto reported to the squadron commander and said, "Sir, the Russians are sending more of their heavy bombers westward, we stopped the advance formations but you know they have an unlimited reserve, our base may be next!"

"Yes I know, the reserve squadrons are already on alert, refresh yourself while you can, you will be back up in the sky shortly," replied Hauptmann Ritter, "there is no rest for any of us!"

Rolf, Ernst, and Hugo went to the cafeteria; they met the remainder of the pilots from their class of replacements. "What is it like, flying wingman with one of the top aces?" One young pilot queried. Others chided in, "Are you learning anything new?"

Rolf answered, "I think I would be dead by now if it were not for Lt. Hans, he is so daring he makes his plane dance to his music!"

Ernst replied, "Lt. Charles is phenomenal, I think he really does have eyes in the back of his head! He sees the enemy that no one else has seen, he ordered me to stick close to him and do as he says without question. I too would be dead if it were not for him."

Hugo added, "I am the luckiest of all, flying with the deputy commander has also trained me to think, Oberlt. Olagande flies as if he was playing chess with the enemy; his maneuvers never fit a pattern. He always outthinks his enemy before his final attack! Whenever I write my father, I always mention Oberlt. Olagande and how he is tutoring me."

Meanwhile in the officer's quarters, Hans and Charles discussed the situation. Hans said, "I am pleased with my wingman, Rolf, he is developing into an instinct fighter pilot. I don't have to tell him what to do; he does what I want him to do without me having to tell him, how is your wingman doing?"

Charles replied, "Fine, he is a little too tight sometimes

but he is improving every day. I tell him not to be too perfect, to let the battle flow before him and adjust accordingly. I notice that Otto's wingman, Hugo, idolizes him, following him everywhere. Otto will make him an experte soon; I believe Hugo has at least seven or eight victories already."

Otto returned to his quarters and mentally prepared for the next battle, he found Hans and Charles and told them, "Rest now, the Russians are on their way with their heavy stuff, they suffered severe losses in their first attempt but to them that is just a temporary setback."

Suddenly the sirens wailed, the command echoed throughout the base, "The Russians are coming, the Russians are coming! All flights take off immediately!"

The expected hordes of Russian bombers approached the air base as the last of the Luftwaffe fighters ascended into the clouds above to give battle. The new Tupolev Tu2 twin-engine bombers accompanied the heavy Petlyakov Pe8 bombers and the Ill-2 'Shturmoviks'; there was also massive fighter escort with the La-5's, the newest Yak-9's and the MiG-3's.

The weather conditions enveloped the entire area in a thick fog and low clouds limiting visibility to a few kilometers. This was not the type of weather that favored fighter pilots.

The Luftwaffe base received the full frenzy of the Russian onslaught. All ground personnel were huddled in the shelters as the bombs rained down destroying everything in sight coupled with the terror of the 'Shturmoviks' raking the area with their cannon fire. As the bombing continued the clashes with the Luftwaffe fighters was undiminished in fury as the Russians pressed home their attack.

After the last bomb fell, the Russian Group Commander shouted over his radio, "Let us return home my comrades, our mission here has been successful! We will celebrate this day!"

They broke off the attack and returned to their bases. From the underground bunker, Oberstleutnant Mueller radioed the surviving pilots and ordered them to land at the nearest bases located in southern Poland, he continued, "The adjutant will give you the coordinates, after making your landing submit your reports and be ready to fly and fight again!"

The pilots, exhausted to the point of collapse, many of them wounded with varying degrees of severity, landed at the scattered Polish airfields, often the damaged planes crashed on impact, adding to the chaos.

Otto directed the remnants of his squadron to a small airfield at the edge of the forest located near the town of Krakow. The accommodations were primitive; the local populace, including the doctors, were rounded up and brought to the airfield to assist the Luftwaffe personnel servicing the pilots as they landed and to care for the wounded. Otto watched anxiously as the planes landed, he became concerned as he watched intently as a Focke-Wulf fighter with a red nose limped in for a rough landing, its engine belching smoke.

Otto whispered to himself, "Charles is in trouble, God help him!" Otto ordered a personnel carrier equipped with a stretcher to drive directly to the plane, assist in evacuating the pilot, and drive the pilot to the emergency aid station. The plane belly-flopped to a landing as flames engulfed the engine. The ground personnel hurriedly extricated Charles from the stricken plane and placed him in the carrier. Otto remained at the airfield until the last planes landed, a Focke-Wulf with an orange nose and two other fighters following close behind. Otto was relieved to see that Hans with his wingman, Rolf, and Ernst, Charles' wingman, had landed safely. Otto told the three that Charles was at the emergency aid station. Otto stated, "When I finish my report to headquarters I will join all of you at the aid station."

Later Otto rushed to the aid station. Hans, Rolf, and Ernst were in conference with the attending physician, as Charles was lying sedated on a cot with three mattresses, serving as a makeshift hospital bed.

When Otto entered the room, the physician introduced himself, "I am Doctor Anton Kalzinski, your pilot has suffered numerous shrapnel wounds to his left arm and left shoulder, he will not be flying for a while. I dressed his wounds but for now he needs rest, taking all the pieces of shrapnel from his wounds will take some time."

Otto thanked the doctor and explained to Hans, Rolf, and Ernst that he needed to find the airbase commander. "I need replacements now and that includes more pilots as well as planes."

The base commander, Oberleutnant Fritz Heller and Otto introduced themselves. "I am pleased to see that you and your personnel had made preparations for our sudden arrival under these intense conditions. I will include in my report how efficiently you were able to marshal the townspeople in caring for my pilots."

Oberlt. Heller replied, "Thank you Herr Olagande, it is my pleasure, I have heard about you and the 'Black Knights' and your 387th Fighter Wing. I envy you and wish I could fight alongside of you but I personally have not been able to fly since being severely wounded in an earlier campaign, the 'Battle of Britain'."

Oberlt. Heller hobbled along with his cane, his thin build bent over but still managing a smile in spite of the pain he suffers from his old wounds.

"I will put a request through to headquarters to have replacement planes delivered as soon as possible but I have my doubts as to any replacement pilots, EVERYONE requests replacement pilots, Herr Olagande!"

The Russian winter gave way to the Russian spring of 1944; heavy cloud cover with blowing snow blanketed the Kharkov sector. The grey overcast, and occasional heavy rain caused an eerie calm throughout the region. Only reconnaissance flights took place during this period. The ground forces on both sides took a temporary pause in the main fighting, the skirmishes and guerilla attacks continued however.

The 387th Fighter Wing moved to a larger air base located east of the oil fields of Ploesti, Rumania. Oberstleutnant Mueller sent orders for the entire Wing, including the mechanics, to assemble at the main hall. The Wing came to attention as Oberstleutnant Mueller ascended to the podium. The Wing Commander announced, "This temporary respite is good news, in spite of the terrible weather, we are being supplied with new planes and replacement parts. Many of my bomber crews will fly the twin engine Me110 attack fighter-bombers. The tactics will change since the 110s are faster, more maneuverable, and more heavily armed than the bombers, they will have a fighting chance against the Russian fighters. These planes will carry out quick bombing raids against selected targets and after that, they will be able to revert to a fighter role. The new Me109s have engines that are more powerful with better superchargers; they also have added two extra machine guns. We already have one such fighter plane, the plane flown by Oberleutnant Olagande; the new Focke-Wulf fighters are the 190-E, greater range and with bomb carrying capabilities. The bad news is there will be no new replacement pilots; the Western Front has top priority on all new pilots! I am ordering all of you to STAY ALIVE!" The Wing Commander then saluted his pilots then left the podium. Cheers erupted, a renewed optimism swept over everyone in the assembly room.

In the days that followed, all pilots familiarized themselves with their new planes, conferring with the mechanics and checking the new engines for more speed. Bomber pilots assigned to the new Me110s, or 'Zerstorer', joyfully checked out their new mounts.

Max mused, "I am going to learn to fly one of these." Max told his rear gunner, "Erik we are going to fly as many reconnaissance missions as possible during this terrible weather with one of these Me110s. We need to get use to the feel of flying these 'mounts', our new role as a fighter unit will be upon us as soon as the weather breaks."

Erik appeared anxious, "I am looking forward to it Sir, we can still kill tanks with the cannons these planes are armed with."

In the enlisted men's quarters, the young pilots discussed how pleased they were to get their new fighters.

Rolf related, "I spent the night sitting in the cockpit of my mount, it felt so comfortable I slept there all night. I can hardly wait for the weather to improve so I can take her up and see just what she can do."

Hugo said, "If only my father, the general, could see me now, if he were here I believe he would insist on flying along with me."

Ernst remarked, "I sat and listened to the engine of my mount being tuned by the chief mechanic, it sounded like such sweet music, I can hear my engine above all other engines. I will make my mount perform just like my flight leader's mount. Incidentally, Lt. Toulon is making a speedy recovery from his wounds, he hopes to fly again by springtime."

Over in the officer's quarters the tone was more somber, these veterans knew what to expect when the weather improved. Otto spent many nights praying to his God, chanting in the language of the Ubo, and holding his 'warrior doll' close to his heart. No one understood the Ubo language but Otto, he found that comforting. He could openly express himself in a loud voice as he vented his anger over the course the war was taking. The friendship between Hans and Charles grew after Charles became wounded, they became more like brothers than just comrades.

Charles confessed in a soft tone, "Hans, I am becoming a 'killing machine', I find myself enjoying sending my adversary to his eternal resting place, I used to enjoy cooking and baking, now all I think about is my next battle, what is happening to me?"

Hans replied, "We all think like that, it is natural to think like that, do not worry." Hans knew that he did not think that way, he was just doing a job and he prided himself as being 'good at his job'.

The spring weather rapidly approached, the clouds thinned and the warm sunshine bathed the entire landscape in its warm glow, the countryside turned green with new foliage, the beauty of nature was everywhere. The ominous reality however was that hostilities would resume soon and everyone along the entire front braced for the coming battle.

Max and Erik honed their skills at flying the Me110; Max practiced firing the heavy array of guns concentrated in the nose of the cockpit. Max commented to Erik, "The power generated by these cannons and machine guns is awesome; a short burst will disintegrate anything before them, we can also destroy tanks with these guns!"

"I am looking forward to testing our new mount in battle, Herr Oberleutnant."

The sirens wailed as the expected attack by hordes of Russian bombers speeded westward toward the German lines! The raid consisted of the giant four-engine heavy bombers, the Petlyakov Pe-8; and the medium bombers, the twin-engine Tupolev Tu-2, and the famous Il-2 'Shturmoviks'. Fighters from the Red Guard Air Division escorted the bombers.

The Luftwaffe scrambled all available fighters to meet the threat! The heavily armed Me110s rose aloft to engage the Russian bombers, they followed the speedier Me109s and FW190s whose primary task was to engage the Russian fighters.

The Me110 squadrons continued to climb into the heavens, high above the altitude of the approaching Russian bombers. The squadrons flew above the whirlwind of the combat in progress between the opposing fighters. Max' squadron was the lead squadron, soon he spotted the Russian bombers, Max shouted into his radio, "Bombers below to the east, ATTACK!" The Me110s peeled off into a steep dive and lined up their prey! The simultaneous roar of cannon and machine gunfire caught the Russians by surprise! Bomber after bomber fell from the sky in flames as the Me110s raked through the bomber formations! The Me110 squadrons infiltrated the bomber stream and attacked repeatedly and relentlessly, as falcons attacking helpless pigeons, until the few surviving bombers fled eastward back toward their bases! Some of the Russian fighters disengaged the Luftwaffe fighters and climbed to meet the Me110s when they became aware of the carnage suffered by the bombers. The Me110s maneuvered for a head-on attack on the climbing Russian fighters. The Russian planes disintegrated when hit by the concentrated fire of the cannons and machine guns. The Me110 strategy was to return to base after dispatching the bombers and not to actively engage the Russian fighters unless attacked.

The Me110 crews landed and reported to the debriefing officer. The films from the gun cameras disclosed results that far exceeded expectations! The tactics used to intercept and destroy the bombers using the Me110s became the 'Order of the Day' throughout the Luftwaffe!

Max' first mission as a fighter pilot netted him and his rear-gunner, Erik, 12 bombers destroyed! Max exclaimed, "I could not believe how much power those guns delivered until I saw my prey disintegrate from my short bursts!" Erik echoed, "What a wild ride we had!"

As the fighters returned, Otto wagged his wings, celebrating his victories. Charles and Hans followed the gesture and wagged their wings, they too had reason to celebrate! After the debriefing Otto, Hans, and Charles grabbed a bottle of champagne and lifted a toast to the pilots and gunners of the Me110 squadrons, their wingmen, Hugo, Rolf, and Ernst, joined in the toast. Otto said, "Max destroyed 12 bombers, they haven't finished the tally of the total number of Russian bombers destroyed. What a victory today!"

The somber side of the equation disclosed the fact there were many pilots that did not return from this gigantic battle and in the upcoming battles, there would be many more pilots that would not return. The Russian fighter pilots from the Red Guard Air Division and other elite divisions were taking their toll of Luftwaffe fighter pilots. There would be increased celebrations at the Russian Fighter Command Headquarters. The headquarters of Russian Bomber Command were devising tactics to avoid the large losses of bombers due to this new threat of the Luftwaffe using their Me110 'Zerstorer' heavy fighter.

During the summer of 1944, the Russian air armadas grew in size, their pilots' skills continued to improve, and their new fighters became more of a match for the Luftwaffe fighters. The Luftwaffe was losing the battle of attrition in pilots, the home front was producing enough planes but the training of a competent fighter pilot took time, a luxury the Luftwaffe could not afford. The replacement pilots' lack of training caused them to become cannon fodder for the opposing fighter forces.

Otto approached Hauptmann Ritter with some news from the Eastern Front, "Herr Hauptmann, some good news for a change, there is a young pilot from the Grunherz (Green Heart) Geschwader that is expected to gain his 300th air victory very soon, and his name is Oberleutnant Erich Hartmann."

"Yes, I have heard of him, it is said the Russians have also placed a bounty on his head, just like in your case."

"I will post this announcement on the bulletin board."

133

As the pilots gathered around the bulletin board and read the announcement, Hans looked at Charles and exclaimed, "Remember the blonde youth we met when we were first transferred to the same squadron?"

"Yes, I remember him, so mannerly, very neat in appearance. Mein Gott, the number 300 is so great, who would think anyone would be close to THAT number."

Chapter

XIII

Adolf Galland,
General of Fighter Command

General of Fighter Command, Adolf Galland, also an 'Ace'
with 102 confirmed Air Victories, all on the Western Front.

On 6 June 1944, the Americans and British opened the Second Front in Europe by landing overwhelming land forces on the beaches of Normandy, France. The Luftwaffe had only two fighters available to oppose the landings on that first day! The Luftwaffe covering the Western European Front had top priority on all newly graduated fighter pilots while the Luftwaffe on the Russian Front had to make do with what was left of their veterans and the younger pilots they had been able to acquire. The Luftwaffe continued to put up stiff resistance against the Russians in spite of the drawbacks.

Max found time to have the black shield with crossed spears painted on his Me110, in addition, he had the face of a shark painted on the nose of the fuselage and the hubs on the propellers of the engines painted deep blue.

Hauptmann Ritter received the remnants of other squadrons added to his depleted squadron. This practice of combining depleted squadrons to form a completed squadron became commonplace at this point in time along the Eastern Front.

Hauptmann Ritter had his pilots assembled and called to attention. He made the following announcement, "The pilots named here will receive promotions: Unteroffizier Rolf Friedland, Unteroffizier Ernst Schiller, and Unteroffizier Hugo von Wassel are promoted to the rank of Leutnant, this order becomes effective immediately. Leutnant Hans Thayer and Leutnant Charles Toulon to the rank of Oberleutnant; this order becomes effective immediately. I have been relieved of my command of this squadron, I am to take command of the entire Wing, and I now have the rank of Oberstleutnant. Finally, your new squadron commander is HAUPTMANN OTTO OLAGANDE! This order becomes effective immediately,

I believe, as well as all of you, that this promotion was long overdue!" The squad room erupted in cheers that resounded all over the base!

Oberstleutnant Ritter continued, "Oberstleutnant Mueller has been transferred to take command of another Wing. I am pleased to announce another promotion; Oberleutnant Max Ule is now Hauptmann Max Ule, squadron commander of the Me110 squadron in which he is serving so valiantly! Hauptmann Schneider has been assigned to command another squadron of Me110s." Again, the squad room erupted in cheers!

Otto and Max met in the cafeteria to have coffee and discuss their promotions and new responsibilities. Wing Commander Ritter also went to the cafeteria; he saw Otto and Max and asked if he could join them, Otto invited him to have a seat.

Commander Ritter said, "We three are now commanders and we will be working closely together from now on, please, I ask both of you to call me Günter, when we are conferring together, there is no time for all the pomp and foolishness. We have served together and have worked well together." Günter extended his hand, all three shook hands on the new relaxed relationship. Günter continued, "I am expecting a visit from the General of All Fighters, Adolf Galland, I will have you two meet him, he has asked about the Black Knights, he will want to meet Hans and Charles also. When he arrives with his staff I will notify both of you." Günter then returned to his office. Otto looked at Max and exclaimed, "I wonder what that is all about!" Max replied, "I have no idea, let us wait and see. By the way, you look good in your new uniform." Both men chuckled after that remark.

Otto had the orderly inform Hans and Charles to

report to his office. Soon Hans and Charles reported. Otto explained, "Both of you be prepared to meet General Adolf Galland, he is coming here to interview us Black Knights. I don't know any more than that, as soon as he arrives both of you will be notified to report to the commander's office."

Later that evening General Galland arrived, he was escorted to the commander's office; there he met Oberstleutnant Günter Ritter, Wing Commander. The Black Knights were summoned to report to the commander's office. After the introductions, General Galland said, "I have heard many stories of you four Black Knights. Back in Berlin most of the Luftwaffe Command staff have no idea you four are Germans of African descent, those of us that know better have remained silent, that subject is so unimportant. My main purpose is to form a Jagdgeschwader Fighter Group, equipped with the new jet fighter, the Messerschmitt 262. I am recruiting the top Luftwaffe Experten fighter pilots to fly this plane and save the Fatherland from these bombing raids on our cities by the American USAAF and the British RAF. The Me262 jet fighter flies at well over 800 km/hr, and its armament consists of four 30mm cannon in the nose, the Allies have nothing that can touch it! The only drawback is the engines are fueled by chemicals; the chemical mixture is very dangerous."

Günter related, "I have heard of such 'wonder weapons' but I have been too busy fighting Russians to give these weapons much thought."

Otto replied, "I too have heard of these jet fighters, I have never seen one, the idea of flying over 800 km/hr sounds fantastic!"

Hans interrupted, "Greetings my General, remember

our chance meeting in Paris four years ago?"

General Galland, exclaimed, "Yes I do, I recognize you now, you look so mature now, not the fresh face young man in his new uniform strutting about, smiling at the pretty mademoiselles along the promenade. Now you are one of the Luftwaffe top experten with over 100 confirmed victories!" General Galland looked at Charles and said, "You must be the Black Knight that has over 180 confirmed 'kills'."

Charles replied, "Yes Sir, 192 at last count."

The General commented, "You have almost twice as many kills as I have, I am proud of you!" General Galland continued, looking at Max, "You must be the fourth Black Knight, former Stuka pilot now Me110 'Zerstorer' pilot, from a tank destroyer to a bomber destroyer."

Max answered, "Yes Sir, I am very honored to meet you."

General Galland looked back at Otto and said, "You are the leader, I can see it in your forbearance, I told many of my staff people that I wanted you in my squadron when I commanded a squadron. Looking at your record, you are still my choice for a staff officer."

Günter interrupted, "Please my General, you are so correct but I need him here, the Russian hordes attack us night and day, with Otto at my side we constantly plan and devise tactics with the minimal forces at my command to meet these threats. In addition, when Otto ascends in his mount to meet the enemy I know we will be victorious."

General Galland laughed, "I did not come here to

disrupt anything. I would take the whole squadron if it were feasible. All of you are valuable to the war effort whatever your assignment. However, I need pilots, good pilots, the cream of the Luftwaffe!"

Otto said, "Sir, I feel honored that you have come here to recruit us. I wish I could clear the skies over our homeland as a member of your 'super squadrons' but without us here to meet the Russian attacks they would crash through our back door! We cannot get any pilots to replace the ones we have already lost nor any replacements for the ones we are sure to lose! However, I can recommend one pilot for your super squadrons, Lt. Hugo von Wassel, son of a Great War cavalry officer, Retired General Albert von Wassel. He is young and dedicated, he has 27 confirmed victories."

Hans added, "There is also Lt. Rolf Friedland, a truly instinctive young fighter pilot with 23 confirmed victories."

Charles related, "What about Lt. Ernst Schiller, a natural with 25 confirmed 'kills', he would fit into the 'jet plane' concept very easily."

Max stated, "Sir, my parents live in Berlin, I would give my life gladly to protect them from harm but I can't leave now, the Russians are advancing toward our homeland as we speak. With my comrades, we will win the war here in Russia together!"

General Galland reached for one of his long cigars and asked, "Do any of you mind if I smoke?" No one objected, the General lit the cigar and puffed slowly.

After a brief moment he spoke, focusing his attention on all four of the 'Black Knights', "Gentlemen please, I can feel the intense loyalty all of you have for each other, like the 'Three Musketeers', 'All for one and one for all', and I respect that. I also know those young men you recommended are your wingmen; I could never break up a fighter pilot and his wingman! I will continue my search elsewhere. Otto, I wish to congratulate you personally for your superb battle with the Soviet Ace, Major Sergei Ostrovanov. That was a classic! In Berlin, they talk of that battle often, comparing it to a western shootout from an American movie."

The General concluded, "Commander Ritter, I thank you for your hospitality, I wish I could stay to fight the Russians with you, but I must go, I envy you, your men are the best!"

After General Galland departed, Günter looked at Otto, Max, Hans, and Charles and said, "I thank all of you." Günter went to his quarters, the four Black Knights then retired to their quarters.

Chapter

XIV

Operation Bagration

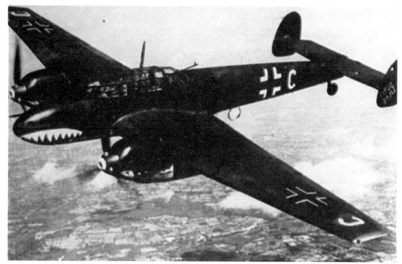

Hauptmann Max Ule flying his Me110C, heavy fighter, known as 'Der Zerstorer' over the Vistula River, Poland, during 'Operation Bagration' September 1944.

As the spring and summer of 1944 progressed, the Russian Armies in the central section advanced to the Vistula River near Warsaw, Poland. In the southern section, the Russian air offensive had amassed a force of over 1200 aircraft against the Luftwaffe's 200 planes to clear the Wehrmacht from the Crimean Peninsula.

Commander Ritter received orders to reinforce the fighter unit commanded by Hauptmann Gerhard Barkhorn, one of the leading fighter aces of the war. The entire armada of Luftwaffe fighters went aloft to blunt the threat of the great air offensive by the Russian Shturmoviks and their fighter escorts against the German artillery positions and the armored units at the rear of the front lines. A furious battle raged between the opposing fighters; however, Otto and his wingman, Hugo, broke through and attacked the rampaging IL-2 Shturmoviks. The sustained attacks of the Black Knights and the many 'experten' fighters of Hauptmann Barkhorn's Jagdgruppe were decimating the Shturmoviks! The Russians did succeed in flushing out the German Wehrmacht defensive positions one by one. The Germans made a hasty withdrawal while under the relentless attack of the Shturmoviks, losing many vehicles and tanks to their withering cannon and machine gun fire! The Me110s arrived on the scene and joined in the melee, Max swept two IL-2s from the sky as he brought his cannons to bear on the attackers. The Me110s and Heinkel 111 bombers attacked the advancing Russian columns of tanks and infantry to relieve the German positions. The Russians brought in additional fighter squadrons consisting of their newer models, the Yak-9s and La-7s! The overwhelming numbers of fighters caused great losses among the He111s. The Luftwaffe's efforts allowed the surviving German ground forces to evacuate the Crimean Peninsula and retreat into Rumania. During the month long battle in the Crimean Peninsula, Commander Ritter's Wing Command sustained losses of over 50% of pilots and planes. In spite of the heavy losses, Charles added 15 victories during the battle, bringing his total to 213! His wingman, Ernst, added 8 IL-2s and 3 Yak-9s to bring his total to 42 victories. Hans added 10 victories, his total was now 176. His wingman, Rolf, added 12 victories, his total now at 41. Otto added 21 victories bringing his total to 195! His wingman, Hugo, added 18 bringing his total to 47 victories. Max destroyed 27 tanks, 24 trucks and 12 artillery batteries! His total tanks destroyed number 353! In addition, Max shot down 14 fighters and bombers, for his total of 32 air victories!

The battle of the Crimean Peninsula was a prelude to the coming battle for central Russia, led by Russia's greatest air offensive, known as 'Operation Bagration'!

'Operation Bagration' was launched on 22 June 1944, the third anniversary of 'Operation Barbarossa', Germany's invasion of Russia. The Russian offensive to clear the central Russian front of the Fourth Army and the Third Panzerarmee was to be spearheaded by waves of Il-2 and the new Il-10 Shturmoviks, the twin-engine Petlyakov Pe-2 dive-bombers, the twin-engine Tupolev Tu-2 medium bombers, and four engine Tupolev/Petlyakov Pe-8 heavy bombers.

Commander Ritter notified the wing they would be operating along the central Russian front supporting the retreat of the Third Panzerarmee. Commander Ritter summoned his squadron commanders to his office, the grim, determined look in his eyes foretold of unpleasant news.

"Gentlemen, the Russians are advancing on every front, they have copied our 'blitzkrieg' tactics with a few improvements! They have amassed endless numbers of attack aircraft, mainly their 'Shturmoviks', escorted by large numbers of their newest fighters. Instead of advancing their tanks, they are leading with their Shturmoviks to blast a path through our lines and attack our artillery positions then they are following with their infantry and tanks. I do not need to remind any of you we will be fighting against overwhelming odds in sheer numbers alone!" Commander Ritter reminded his pilots, "Our tactics will be to attack the Shturmoviks and bombers primarily, then their fighters! If there are no questions then be prepared to take off immediately!"

Otto grimly told Max, "This battle will be extra dangerous for you heavy 'Zerstorer' fighters; we will do our very best to protect you, kill as many of those Shturmoviks as you can!"

Max replied, "No need to worry, I am invincible!" Max with his rear gunner, Erik, sprinted to their Me110 and took off.

After all planes were aloft Commander Günter Ritter returned to his office and pored over the maps, studying the details of the Russian and German positions. In a subdued tone he uttered, "The position is very grave! If we do not stop this Russian offensive we will be fighting on German soil very soon!"

The Luftwaffe fighters droned on until they observed in the distance billows of smoke rising from the killing fields, the swarms of Russian bombers and the tank busting Shturmoviks circling around the German positions. Each Luftwaffe pilot strained his mount to close as fast as possible, in an instant the opposing forces were engaged in fierce combat! The Russian fighters intercepted the Luftwaffe fighters to thwart the Luftwaffe effort to engage the bombers and Shturmoviks as they rained destruction on the German troops below.

In the melee, one plane among the hundreds of combatants was observed spiraling to earth in flames, a yellow-nose Messerschmitt Me109, the mount of Hauptmann Otto Olagande! Two Russian Yak-9 pilots followed the Me109 in its dive, one of the Russian pilots exclaimed over his radio, "We shot down one of the Black Knights! We are going to finish him off!" Those were the last words to come from that pair of Russian pilots. The guns of two Focke-Wulf 190s delivered withering gunfire to these hapless Russians, destroying them! Otto's wingman, Lt. Hugo von Wassel, and fellow Black Knight, Oblt. Charles Toulon, were the pilots who flew these planes.   The stricken Me109 belly-landed in a marsh and came to rest in a shallow lake. Otto Olagande opened the canopy and jumped into the water as the flaming wreck descended into the waters. Otto swam away under water as troops were approaching, he did not know if the troops were German or Russian, he was taking no chances. Otto finally surfaced and continued to swim until he decided it was safe to leave the lake. Crawling through the bushes, he stopped to check his bearings; he traveled westward hoping to reach the German lines. As darkness came, Otto checked his Luger automatic pistol before resting. Otto could hear the distant thunder of explosions from the intense shelling and see the brilliant flashes of light in the night skies as the battle raged on, wearily he curled among some bushes and attempted to sleep. As dawn approached, Otto awakened, shivering in the cold, still wet from his ordeal of swimming in the lake. He started walking through the marsh until he came to the edge of a forest. After going deeper into the forest, he could hear voices. Otto stopped and drew his pistol; stealthily he crept toward the area where the voices were coming from. When he got closer, he could hear the voices talking in Russian. Looking through the bushes he could see there were at least ten men, armed with rifles and machine guns, he had stumbled upon a

Russian partisan guerrilla camp! One of the men was operating a radio while another was studying a map, the rest were sitting around a small fire. Otto surmised the partisans were radioing German troop movements in the area, which meant he was close to the German lines. Another group of six men joined this group. They were leading horses packed with supplies. Otto strained to hear the conversation as one, apparently the leader, explained to the others they had to destroy two bridges in the vicinity to prevent the German troops from escaping while the Russian army encircled them. Otto could see the supplies were explosives as they were distributed among the men.

The men moved quietly through the forest until they approached the bridges, Otto stealthily followed close behind. From his vantage point, Otto could see German sentries posted at the bridges. Otto had to alert the sentries before the partisans could sneak up and kill them! Otto carefully aimed his pistol at one of the sentries and fired. The bullet struck the sentry and he yelled, "Alarm! Alarm!" The other sentries responded at once and a pitched battle erupted between them and the partisans! Otto laid in ambush for the radio operator as he set up his radio. Two quick shots immediately dispatched the radio operator; Otto grabbed the radio operator's machine gun and opened fire on the partisans nearest him, the partisans discovered they were in the crossfire between Otto and the sentries! The remainder of the partisans escaped into the forest. When the firing subsided, Otto stood up with his arms raised high and shouted, "Comrade!" The sentries approached cautiously and ordered Otto to advance slowly. When they could see Otto in the dim light, they were amazed to see this German officer standing before them, in his crumpled dirty uniform! They marched Otto to the guardhouse where the commanding officer, Lt. Karl Franken, and the other sentries stared in amazement. Lt. Franken spoke, "Who are you? Where did you come from? You are a Luftwaffe officer, what are you doing here?"

Otto responded, "I am Hauptmann Otto Olagande, assigned to the 387th Fighter wing, I was shot down 20 to 30km east of here two days ago and stumbled upon Russian partisan guerrillas that had planned to blow up these two bridges. Alert your commanding officer at once, all the troops in this area are in danger of encirclement by the Russian army! The partisans had planned to cut off your retreat as soon as the Russian army begins their offensive in this area!"

Lt. Franken stared in disbelief; he demanded proof of Otto's identity. Otto produced his identification papers then demanded that Lt. Franken notify his superior officer immediately! Lt. Franken called his unit's headquarters and notified them of the imminent threat. Lt. Franken told Otto, "Sir, the commanding officer is sending a detachment to bring you to headquarters; he would like to personally interview you. I told him you were in need of cleaning up, that you were extremely dirty and grimy. I also told him you helped us save the bridges by killing some of the partisans before they escaped."

Otto arrived at the unit's field headquarters; there he met Colonel Franz Lantz, the commanding officer of the 54th Infantry Battalion. Col. Lantz had his orderly prepare a bath for Otto and to clean Otto's uniform. After the bath, Otto was given a robe while his uniform was being cleaned.

Col. Lantz was speechless when Otto reported to him in full uniform. He observed that Otto's skin color remained a deep brown even after his bath!

Col. Lantz regained his composure and inquired, "You are a Luftwaffe fighter pilot?"

"Yes Sir, I am Hauptmann Otto Olagande, 387th Fighter Wing, I command a squadron. I was shot down east of here but I managed to evade the Russians. I was hiding in the forest in my attempt to reach our lines when I came upon Russian partisan guerrillas who had planned to destroy the two bridges at your rear. I alerted your sentries and we successfully saved the bridges. I had to shoot one of your sentries however to get their attention, I hope the wound is not serious."

Col. Lantz exclaimed, "That was brilliant thinking, I will note that in my report!"

One of Col. Lantz' staff entered the room with a communique and handed it to Col. Lantz. Col. Lantz read it and gasped, "This communique states you are the famous 'Black Knight' squadron leader, one of the top leading aces of the Luftwaffe, thought to be missing in action along the central front!" Col. Lantz continued, "I am honored to meet you, we down here on the ground often follow the careers of you fighter pilots, we fantasize about your exploits! I will notify your unit immediately that you are safe and I shall expedite your swift return to your squadron! You lead a charmed life!"

Otto thought silently as he fondled his warrior doll, "Thank you mother for your ever present protection."

Col. Lantz related to Otto, "You are my honored guest, anything I can do for you please let me know and it shall be done. In the meantime, I must prepare for our Russian 'friends'."

Col. Lantz and his battalion crossed the bridges,

escaping the Russian armored column sent after them; Col. Lantz then ordered the bridges blown up, living to fight another day!

Chapter

XV

A Hero's Return

Hauptmann Otto Olagande flying his new Me109G after his return to his unit.

Meanwhile back at the 387th Fighter Wing news of Otto's survival brought cheers and thanksgivings from everyone, especially Wing Commander Ritter and Lt. Hugo von Wassel, Otto's wingman. Hans, Charles and Max gathered in Otto's quarters and chanted prayers in Swahili for the 'Enchanted Life' and the safe return of their comrade. There was great concern for Otto's safety as news of a huge battle of Col. Lantz' battalion against overwhelming odds reached Luftwaffe Headquarters Central. Two days after being engaged in heavy ground fighting with Col. Lantz' infantry battalion Otto received transport back to the 387th Fighter Wing and his comrades, Otto received a hero's welcome on his safe return. A new Me109 was waiting for Otto on his return, Otto was surprised to see the black shield with crossed spears and the bright yellow nose already painted on his mount.

At the roll call for all 387th Fighter Wing personnel Commander Ritter presented Otto with his new plane and read the commendation for Otto saving an infantry battalion from annihilation by the partisan guerrillas and the Russian army. General of Fighters Adolf Galland arrived and presented Otto with the Knight's Cross of the Iron Cross! After the ceremony, General Galland told Otto, "I wish you would return with me to Berlin but at the same time I am glad you are here to help stop the Russians." Otto smiled and told the General, "I understand and I am honored."

There was a gathering of Hans, Charles, Max and Hugo in Otto's quarters as they inquired about the Russian who had shot Otto down.

Otto related, "The Russian was very good, I did not see him at first, I was busy chasing a 'Shturmovik' when he closed and let me have it."

Otto joked, "I needed eyes in the back of my head like you Charles!" The room erupted in subdued laughter.

Hugo asked Otto, "Sir, What did I do wrong? I am your wingman and it is my duty to protect you at all times even at the cost of my own life!"

Otto replied, "Hugo, you did nothing wrong, you did protect me, there were two other Russians closing on me and when they saw you they fled only to die from your guns."

Otto turned grim as he spoke of his brief interlude with Col. Lantz' battalion, "Col. Lantz assigned a squad to protect me while we were retreating from the Russians and I told him that I would fight at his side, for him to save his troops for the main fighting. Col Lantz refused, he said I was more valuable fighting for him and his men up in the sky than down on the ground!"

After a brief moment to regain his composure, Otto continued, "Gentlemen, I have a profound respect for those brave soldiers that fight ground battles. I must relate to you one of my experiences." Again a moment of silence, then Otto spoke, "The soldiers in my squad carried a belt-fed machine gun, I helped by carrying two canisters of belt ammunition. A forward Russian patrol intercepted us and attacked, the entire squad was killed for the exception of the soldier who carried the machine gun! He fell to the ground and quickly moved into a crouched position, he cradled the gun in his arms and ordered me to feed the belts of ammo through his gun as he pointed it and fired! He fired continuously until we were out of ammunition!"

Otto paused and reached for a handkerchief. He then spoke after wiping his brow, "In front of us were the piles of bodies of dead Russian troops, close enough for us reach out and touch! The rest of the Russian patrol retreated into the forest when reinforcements from Col. Lantz' battalion arrived! I salute those soldiers; very seldom do we as pilots get to see directly into our enemy's eyes as we are engaged in combat! That infantry soldier and I did, he did not flinch for one moment, he was magnificent! His hands and forearms became burned from holding that red hot smoking gun! I sent a detailed report of that engagement to Col. Lantz; I want that soldier to be acknowledged and rewarded for his deed!"

Everyone in the room sat spellbound as Otto spoke. The room remained silent after he concluded his story.

Hans broke the silence, "We think only of ourselves most of the time, forgetting the hell other fighting men go through."

Max agreed, "Yes, we do seem to think only of our own suffering."

Charles added, "Otto, we thank God for returning you safe and sound."

Hugo mumbled, "Amen!"

Suddenly the sirens sounded, Otto yelled, "All personnel to the assembly hall!" Commander Ritter was already at the podium. The drone of engines starting up filled the air with their ominous humming; the glow of fire from their exhausts cast a scene likened to fireflies on this cool, crisp night.

Commander Ritter stated grimly, "The Russians are committing a huge force of bombers and Shturmoviks to our area, our early warning system picked them up coming directly toward us, they must be coming to destroy our airbase! Take off immediately!"

Every plane took off into the dark blue night sky, every pilot focused on destroying the Russian attack!

Otto gunned his new mount skyward; he could feel the surge of power of his turbo-charged engine rocketing him into the heavens! Otto shouted over his radio, "My fellow eagles, this is our day of reckoning, onward to destroy the enemy!"

Max and his squadron of Me110s circled high above the airfield to intercept any bombers that were able to break through.

The night sky had an eerie glow from a half-moon and countless stars, a night such as this has often been referred to as a 'bomber's moon'. As the Luftwaffe fighters sped toward the formations of Russian bombers, every pilot was awed at such a beautiful scene and that this could be his last night before joining the legion of countless fallen comrades!

A voice from the lead squadron broke radio silence and shouted, "Alert! Russian fighters ahead!"

The forward squadrons engaged the Russian fighters while Otto and his squadrons circled around the Russians then dived on the bomber squadrons.

Otto exclaimed, "This is a massive effort, there must be well over two hundred bombers heading toward our base! We need reinforcements!"

Otto patted the dashboard of his new fighter and said in a loving voice, "I am christening you tonight my beauty, soon you shall taste Russian bombers for breakfast!" The staccato of cannon fire and machine gun fire from Otto's guns claimed his first victim of the night! Following close to Otto's side was Hugo who opened fire with his guns and he too claimed his first victim of the night! In the melee that followed the flaming corpses of bombers and Shturmoviks fell from the skies as Otto's squadrons flew within the bomber stream dispatching death and destruction! Rear formations of Russian fighters engaged Otto and his squadrons in an effort to chase Otto and his squadrons from the Russian bombers as they pressed ever forward! The overwhelming numbers of Russian fighters were taking their toll of the Luftwaffe fighters; many an 'eagle' would fly and fight no more!

As the bombers approached the Luftwaffe airfield, Max and his formations of Me110s dived into the bomber stream, raking the bombers with the withering fire from their heavy guns! The Russians ignored their losses and lined up their targets. They dropped their bombs, destroying hangars, warehouses, and the fuel storage tanks, causing huge fires to rage! The Shturmoviks came in low and strafed trucks, parked planes and any other targets of opportunity! Other Russian fighters broke off from combat and assisted in strafing the airfield, causing further destruction!

The loud booming voice of the Russian Group Commander shouted over his radio, "Let us go home my comrades, our mission here has been successful! The enemy no longer has his home on Russian soil!"

The remaining Russian bombers and fighters then turned eastward and headed back toward their bases. The Russians soon celebrated their stunning victory over the Luftwaffe this night!

Chapter

XVI

The Inglorious Retreat
Back to the Fatherland

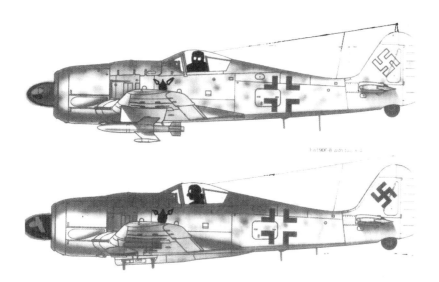

Oberlts. Hans Thayer and Charles Toulon flying their new
Focke-Wulf Fw-190F-8's with rocket launchers toward the
Ploesti Oil Fields, Rumania, January 1945.

Commander Ritter climbed out of the shelter and surveyed the widespread destruction to the airfield and its facilities, he hurriedly summoned the radio operator and in a grim voice shouted, "Instruct all pilots to land their planes at other airfields located near Ploesti. Upon landing, they are to make their reports immediately!" Commander Ritter then assembled all surviving base personnel and ordered, "Prepare to evacuate at once! Transportation is coming to take whatever we can salvage; we will be relocating to a temporary base further west, anything we cannot take, DESTROY!"

Otto directed his squadron to a small airfield located east of the oil fields of Ploesti. Otto remained at his station as the planes landed. There was a long wait, 15 minutes, before more planes arrived and landed. Otto strained as he looked skyward, looking for a fighter with an orange nose! Otto muttered in a whisper, "Where is Hans?" Soon two planes appeared on the horizon, one with an orange nose! Otto was relieved, after the two planes landed Otto went over to the two pilots, Hans and his wingman, Rolf. Otto asked, "What kept you two so long?"

Hans replied, "Rolf saw a straggler, an Il-10 Shturmovik, and we had to bring it down. Rolf deserves the credit; I covered for him while he attacked."

In a joyous tone Otto said, "Good show, I wish we could have swept the sky clear of all of them. Charles and his wingman, Ernst, have already landed, they are with the debriefing officer." After all the planes were accounted for Otto rushed to the makeshift office of the debriefing officer, he made inquiries as to the status of Wing Commander Günter Ritter and the 387th Fighter Wing Airfield.

The reports stated the Commandant had survived and

the 387th Fighter Wing's new assignment would be the large airdrome at Breslau, Germany. Otto gasped, "We are going home!" Otto pored over the reports and was relieved to know that Max was alive and well, that he lost only two planes from his squadron. The news concerning the fate of the 54th Infantry Battalion was devastating. The communique described how the battalion fought to the last man against overwhelming odds in preventing the Russian army from crossing the Vistula River at Warsaw, Poland, their actions allowed the bulk of the Third Panzerarmee to escape a Russian pincers encirclement. The news mentioned that their commander, Col. Lantz, was cited posthumously for his actions. The Citation stated in part, "The heroic action of Col. Franz Lantz in leading his battalion in a pitched battle at the Vistula River near Warsaw, Poland, against the bridgehead of an enemy of overwhelming strength, his actions halted their advance thus allowing the bulk of the Third Panzerarmee to escape a pincer's encirclement. This recommendation for the presentation of the Knight's Cross with Oak Leaves and Crossed Swords is to be awarded to Col. Franz Lantz, posthumously, for his extreme bravery and gallantry in the face of the enemy."

"What a brave warrior," Otto sighed as he recalled recently being with Col. Lantz and his 54th Infantry Battalion when they guarded him to insure his safe return back to his squadron, "I cannot describe how much I owe the Colonel and his wonderful soldiers for my being here, safe and sound, today."

Otto called for a command car to take him to the airfield where Max and his squadron had landed. As the car pulled in front of the airfield office Max came out to greet his comrade.

"What a fight, where did the Russians get all those planes?" Max inquired.

Otto answered, "Intelligence warned us of the Russian Air Force buildup months ago but no one listened! Max, I have news of our new destination; it is the airdrome near Breslau. We are going home!"

Max replied, "That sounds like bad news, although I will be happy to be back in Germany where at least I can sleep at night without the thought of waking up and looking at a Russian soldier standing over my bed with his gun pointed at me!"

Otto related, "Yes, the news is bad, the Russians are advancing everywhere, pushing us back into our homeland! I am awaiting orders from our commander; they had to hurriedly abandon our air base after the Russians leveled everything!"

Max asked, "How bad were your losses?"

Otto stated, "Terrible!"

An orderly approached Otto and Max with a communique from Commander Ritter. Otto read it and told Max, "We have to gather the planes and pilots we have left and assemble them for an attack on an advancing column of Russian armor coming through southern Poland. The coordinates of the attack will follow in the next communique."

Max said, "You must join me for lunch before you return to your airfield, you look very fatigued."

"I will take some food for my driver and me, I must return immediately." Otto and his driver then rushed to his airfield.

When Otto approached his airfield the planes were lined

up on the tarmac, pilots were rushing to their planes; engines were revving up, Otto signaled from his command car for the planes to take off! The fighters soared skyward; Otto hurried to his quarters and donned his flight suit. Otto soon had his plane climbing to join his squadron, in the distance he observed Max and his squadron of Me110s climbing to follow. All pilots were relieved to see the bright yellow nose Me109 in the formation. The rest of the 387th Wing joined the squadrons of Otto and Max as they sped eastward.

Heavy clouds hovered above the ground obscuring targets below; Max and his Me110 'Zerstorer' squadron approached the area at ground level, reasoning that the Russians planes above could not see them speeding toward the Russian armored column until it was too late. Max broke radio silence and shouted, "The tanks are ahead, fire at will!" The staccato of the cannons ripping apart the forward tanks and trucks and the machine guns mowing down the supporting infantry caught the Russian armored units by surprise! Above the clouds, the Russian fighters were already engaged with the Luftwaffe fighter squadrons, unable to disengage and protect the armored column below!

Elated, Max yelled over the radio, "The tanks are destroyed and burning!"

The news reached the airfields used by the 387th Wing; there were cheers shouted throughout the command. Finally, the battle phased out and the planes returned to the small makeshift airfields.

On landing, Otto rushed to the office and sent a preliminary report to Commander Ritter who then forwarded the report to Luftwaffe Command Center. Luftwaffe Headquarters realized that these victories would occur less frequently as the Luftwaffe losses mounted. Replacements were almost non-existent as both pilots and planes were needed on the Western Front to fight and defend the Fatherland as the American Air Force and the RAF combined to bomb German cities to rubble! The Russians were also winning the battle of attrition, The Russians had no regard for suffering heavy losses; they were willing to sacrifice men and materiel to accomplish the mission. The Russians resupplied their air armada with an unlimited amount of new and improved aircraft, in addition, they continued to train and commit new pilots, in vastly increasing numbers, to the offensive!

During the autumn of 1944, from August to October, the Russian offensive relentlessly grinded forward. One 'good' news report was that Oberleutnant Erich Hartmann had achieved his 300th victory, on that date, 25 August, after he had shot down 10 Russians within 50 minutes! Oberlt. Hartmann would receive the Knights Cross with Oak Leaves and Crossed Swords with Diamonds for his amazing feat. By the War's end, Erich Hartmann would have achieved the astonishing total of 352 air victories! He was the highest scoring Ace, from any country, during the Great War.

The Balkan States; Rumania, Hungary, and Bulgaria surrendered to the Russian armies then joined forces with the Russians against the Wehrmacht in the south. On the central front, the Russians advanced into the Baltic States, occupying Lithuania, Latvia, and Estonia. During the month of December, Finland finally surrendered to the Russian armies, removing Germany's ally in the north. The conclusion of 'Operation Bagration' was that, overall, it was a huge strategic success for Russia!

As the Russian winter of 1944-45 began, air activity along the entire front, from Leningrad to the Ukraine, slowed due to heavy cloud cover, snow blizzards, freezing mist and fog that greatly obscured visibility.

The pilots of the 387th Wing, assembled at their new base at Breslau, welcomed the respite. Oblt. Charles Toulon remarked, "This is no way to return home, this is an inglorious retreat!"

Lt. Ernst Shiller chimed in, "I hate coming home like this, like whipped dogs."

Oblt. Hans Thayer and his wingman, Lt. Rolf Friedland, flew reconnaissance missions over the central sector during this time. Commander Ritter conferred with his squadron leaders to assess their strength for the action that was sure to come as soon as the weather cleared.

The squadron of Me110s commanded by Hauptmann Max Ule reported its status at near full strength, as were all the other Me110 squadrons. The Me110 squadrons were on full alert pending any ground activity by Russian armored units.

The squadron of Hauptmann Otto Olagande reported a less than 50% capacity; the other fighter squadrons reported similar statistics. Consolidation plans were submitted to Luftwaffe Headquarters. The new tank-busting fighters, the Focke-Wulf 190 F-8s, were added to the Wing. These fighters were employed with the newest anti-tank weapons, the 'Panzerschreck' anti-tank rockets.

On 16 January 1945, the weather finally cleared. All available aircraft, both Russian and German, were sent into the air. The new FW-190 F-8s flew directly to the Russian tank columns that had been reported in the area, seven tanks were destroyed in the fighter's first passes! However, the FW-190s were pounced by Russian fighters that suddenly appeared like a swarm of locusts, two of the FW-190s were shot down. The remainder of the rocket-carrying fighters escaped the Russian pursuit. The news of the success of the rocket launched shells to destroy hard targets such as tanks spread throughout the Eastern Front. The Russians soon developed their own rocket launchers and armed their Shturmoviks with this new weapon.

The Russian offensive along the Central Front gained momentum as the attacks by squadrons of their Pe-2 dive-bombers and Shturmoviks wreaked havoc on the German artillery positions and forward tank columns!

Following the capture of Warsaw, the Russian army, commanded by General Rokossovsky, was diverted northwards to reach the Baltic shore and isolate East Prussia from the rest of Germany. The Wehrmacht rushed reinforcements from the south to prevent this but these troops were delayed when they encountered another Russian army, led by Marshal Zhukov!

On 20 January 1945, elements of General Konyev's First Ukrainian army crossed the German border at Namslau. On this same day, the 11th Red Guards Army joined the battle in the north and with massive air support; the Russian offensive crossed the border into East Prussia!

The 387th Wing, now a part of Luftflotte 6, engaged the Russian bombers, Shturmoviks, and their numerically superior fighter cover. During the raging battles, the Luftwaffe lost highly experienced pilots such as Oblt. Gustav Schubert, holder of the Knight's Cross with Oak Leaves, destroyer of over 70 Russian tanks; Ofw. Hans Ludwig, another tank-busting ace with at least 85 tanks destroyed; and Gruppenkommandeur Major Ernst-Christian Reusch, holder of the Knight's Cross, and the commander of II./SG 1 Fighter Assault Group!

In the south, the Russians established a bridgehead on German soil after crossing the Oder River at Oppeln, southeast of Breslau, other crossings of the Oder River soon followed. The situation was critical, the Luftwaffe finally received pilot reinforcements from the Western Front and with the addition of more planes, including the new FW-190 F-8s, the Luftwaffe gained air superiority for the first time since 1942. The Luftwaffe flew over 3300 combat sorties on the Eastern Front between 31 January and 2 February.

The 387th Fighter Wing received more of the FW-190 F-8 fighter planes. Hauptmann Otto Olagande held roll call, he instructed the squadrons, including the new pilot replacements, on the order of battle.

Otto announced, "A new weather front is moving in fast, it is bringing a raging storm with heavy downfalls of rain intermingled with snow, the report states a thaw will soon follow. The smaller dirt roads will become impassable quagmires, making the movement of tanks, trucks, and even horse drawn vehicles come to a halt! The Russians will have to use the few hard surface concrete roads for their long supply columns. The tanks and other vehicles crammed on these roads and highways will prove a bonanza for our roaming fighters and bombers, especially the rocket firing fighters. DRIVE THESE BASTARDS FROM GERMAN SOIL!"

The planes took off and soon came upon Russian infantry units south of the city of Kustrin making their way across the frozen land. The planes bombed and strafed the hapless troops, turning the scene into a killing zone! Other planes raced to the roads loaded with Russian tanks, trucks and other vehicles.

Lt. Hugo von Wassel was flying one of the FW-190 F-8s; he laughed hysterically as he dove on the endless column, firing his rockets, causing flaming wrecks in his wake! Following close behind were Lts. Rolf Friedland and Ernst Schiller, also flying FW-190 F-8s.

Rolf exclaimed, "I blew up a 'Stalin' tank! Unbelievable!"

Ernst chimed in, "Look at all the explosions, we are destroying them!"

Hauptmann Max Ule and his squadrons of Me110s swept down on the Russian artillery positions, with their sustained cannon and machine gun fire they wreaked havoc among the crews, silencing the big guns. Max' squadrons veered off and attacked the improvised airfields the Russians prepared near their front lines, catching many planes on the ground. The herculean efforts of the Luftwaffe caused the Russian offensive along the Vistula-Oder Front to slow then stall. The rising temperatures as spring approached thawed the frozen ground and produced thick muddy roads that also attributed to the slowing of the Russian offensive.

Commander Günter Ritter conferred with Otto concerning the present fuel supplies, he said, "Otto, we have stalled the Russian offensive by our tenacious actions but we cannot sustain our efforts due to the lack of fuel! The dwindling fuel stocks have made it necessary to disband some of the fighter operations! Our garrison is fighting for its life at this moment, the Russians are attempting to encircle Breslau but we are holding them off for now, the situation is grave!"

Otto listened silently and then responded, "They are headed to Berlin, hope is fading fast."

During a respite in the air warfare, Otto gathered Hans, Charles, and Max together; Otto directed them to the mess hall for their usual 'cup of coffee conference'.

Otto related, "The news is very grim, the Russians have entered the outskirts of Berlin, I know what this news mean to you Max, your parents still living there, and..."

An orderly rushed into the mess hall shouting, "THE FUEHRER IS DEAD! THE FUEHRER IS DEAD! MORE NEWS TO FOLLOW!"

The date was 30 April 1945! All four Black Knights stared at each other in total disbelief! Hugo, Rolf, and Ernst burst into the mess hall, ran over to the Black Knight's table, and asked, "Is it true?" "What does this mean?"

Commander Ritter entered the mess hall and firmly stated, "It is true! The Fuehrer is dead! He died in his underground bunker in Berlin, no other news yet but I will announce to everyone when I receive the updated details!"

The latest official report stated the Fuehrer died by his own hand and later that night the Russians planted the Red Banner on the Reichstaghaus. The next day German resistance in Berlin crumbled; General Weidling surrendered the city of Berlin to the Russians on 2 May 1945 at 0600 hrs, the 'Battle of Berlin' was over!

The entire 387th Wing assembled for an attack on the Russian forces moving toward Prague, Czechoslovakia.

The Black Knights and their wingmen flew into the Russian bomber formations, fighting past the Russian fighters until they confronted the Russian bombers and Shturmoviks.

Otto shouted over his radio in Swahili, "DEATH TO THE ENEMY!" Charles, Hans, and Max echoed the chorus! The guns of planes bearing the Black Shield with Crossed Spears, their noses painted bright yellow, bright orange, red, and deep blue, blasted their enemy from the skies on this date, 8 May 1945, the last great air battle on the Eastern Front!

News spread throughout the front that THE WAR WAS OVER! The terms of Unconditional Surrender were signed by Germany in the presence of the Allies, The United States of America, Great Britain, France, and Russia on 7 May 1945 at 0241 hrs at Rheims, Germany.

When the squadrons returned to base, they were apprised of the terms of surrender. Many of the pilots openly wept at hearing the news.

Otto announced, "I will never surrender my plane, I have ordered it destroyed!" Hans, Charles and Max agreed unanimously, "Our planes will be destroyed also!"

Commander Ritter had the Wing assemble in the main hall; he went to the podium and addressed the pilots, mechanics, his staff, and all other personnel.

"The Russians are sending a delegation to our airfield, they are to arrive at 0800 hrs tomorrow morning, everyone will wear their dress uniform but do not wear your decorations, they will be kept safe in my office along with your commendations. All hostilities shall cease immediately! The War is over!"

Chapter

XVII

Prisoners of War

In the distance, a Russian tank column approached the 387th Wing airbase as the early hours of dawn bathed the landscape in golden rays of sunshine.

Commander Ritter had all personnel assembled in the main hall; at 0745 hrs, he called everyone to attention. A Russian command car pulled up in front of the headquarters building at 0750 hrs; at 0800hrs, the Russian delegation entered the main hall. Commander Ritter saluted the Russian in command, General Vladimir Kartov, commander of the Fifth Red Guard Tank Army. General Kartov returned the salute.

He approached Commander Ritter and asked, "Is this your whole command?"

Commander Ritter replied, "Yes Sir, this is my entire command."

General Kartov stated, "They can stand at ease, I wish to confer with you in your office."

Commander Ritter gave the command, "Parade rest!" and then retired to his office with General Kartov and the general's adjutant, Col. Ivan Kanyevev.

Gen. Kartov inquired, "Are the four officers with brown skin color, which are standing in the ranks, German?"

Commander Ritter replied, "Yes, they are German, those four officers are the famous 'Black Knights', known throughout the Eastern Front campaign, they are of African descent."

Col. Kanyevev intervened, "Then one of them is the fighter pilot who killed Major Sergei Ostrovanov in air combat, a duel to the death in the skies west of Kharkov in 1943! Major Ostrovanov was one of our leading aces at that time and had been appointed a 'Hero of the Soviet Union'."

Commander Ritter added, "Three of the Black Knights were fighter pilots throughout the conflict, serving on both the Western Front as well as the Eastern Front. They are credited with over 600 air victories collectively and the forth Black Knight, who also served on all fronts, destroyed over 375 tanks, and countless trucks and other vehicles."

Gen. Kartov exclaimed, "I must report this to my superiors! Commander Ritter, there are trucks parked outside to transport your men to our prisoner-of-war compounds, have them board the trucks! You and the four Black Knights will accompany me to our headquarters; have your staff gather all your records and personnel files, we will leave at 1000 hrs."

Commander Ritter called his men to attention and announced, "We are now designated as Prisoners-of-War, and according to the terms of the Geneva Convention, we are to be interred. Gather your gear and board the trucks parked outside! Hauptmann Otto Olagande, Hauptmann Max Ule, Oblts. Charles Toulon and Hans Thayer take seats! The members of my staff are to collect our records, files, and awards and await a command car to take the rest of us to the headquarters of the Fifth Red Guard Tank Army! The rest of you are dismissed; it has been an honor to have been your commander, good luck to all of you!"

After everyone left the hall and boarded the trucks, Commander Ritter approached The Black Knights and stated, "Gen. Vladimir Kartov and his adjutant, Col. Ivan Kanyevev, will take us to his headquarters after my staff has completed their assignment. We can now go to the mess hall for a last cup of coffee."

The five men silently retired to the mess hall, and for the last time, sat at their 'personal' table. An orderly brought the men coffee and strudel cakes.

Hans broke the silence, "Now what?"

Commander Ritter said, "I have no idea, the general seemed very interested in the fact he had the famous 'Black Knights' in his custody, we shall soon see what is in store."

Gen. Kartov invited Commander Ritter and the Black Knights to ride with him and Col. Kanyevev during the journey to the Fifth Red Guard Tank Army Headquarters. The other command car with Commander Ritter's staff followed closely behind, three T-34 tanks escorted the cars to the headquarters. No one spoke during the entire journey.

A cadre of intelligence officers met the entourage of Gen. Kartov after arriving at the headquarters. Commander Ritter and his staff were led away to another building; the Black Knights were taken to a hall where movie and still camera operators and reporters had gathered. Gen. Kartov ordered the Russian soldiers guarding the four Black Knights to take them to the office of Col. Kanyevev and that no shackles or handcuffs were to be applied to the prisoners.

Gen. Kartov then ascended to the podium and announced to all personnel present, "We are to be honored today; the Supreme Commander, Marshal Georgiy Zhukov, and Political Commissar Nikita Khrushchev are scheduled to arrive within the hour to review our troops!

Col. Kanyevev will now conduct the rest of this roll call!"

Gen. Kartov and the intelligence officers then retired to his office.

Gen. Kartov related to the commander of the intelligence officers, Major Aleksandr Osky, "The records of these prisoners are at your disposal. I want to have a comprehensive report on each of them placed on my desk before the arrival of our esteemed guests, I am sure the fate of these prisoners, the Luftwaffe's famous Black Knights, will be decided by them."

Maj. Osky replied, "I fully understand Sir, the reports will be ready in time." Maj. Osky and his staff left Gen. Kartov to engage in their assignment. Gen. Kartov returned to the assembly hall as the troops were preparing for inspection.

Gen Kartov told Col. Kanyevev, "The Black Knights are in your office under guard, I have informed Supreme Headquarters they are in our custody, and Maj. Osky will have detailed reports on our prisoners' records ready and available before the arrival of Marshal Zhukov and Commissar Khrushchev."

Sirens wailed as the motorcade of the Supreme Commander approached Gen. Kartov's headquarters. All troops were in parade formation standing at attention as the Supreme Commander exited his command car. The cameras recorded every moment and the reporters wrote in detail the arrival and the reviewing of the troops. After the ceremony Marshal Zhukov, accompanied by Commissar Khrushchev, were escorted to Gen. Kartov's office.

Commissar Khrushchev inquired, "I understand we

have the Black Knights in custody, is that true?"

"Yes Commissar, that is true," replied Gen. Kartov, "I have their records here, their exploits are very impressive. They have been in the thick of battle from the beginning of the war until the end; they fought on all fronts, from Poland, France, England, and Norway to Africa and the Mediterranean."

Marshal Zhukov interrupted, "Have them brought before me now, I wish to see these 'supermen'!"

The Black Knights were marched into Gen. Kartov's office. Gen. Kartov instructed them to identify themselves. Otto stepped forward and snapped to attention.

"I am Hauptmann Otto Olagande, commander of Fighter Squadron 7A, 387th Wing Command, Luftflotte 6A!"

Otto stepped back and Max stepped forward and snapped to attention.

"I am Hauptmann Max Ule, commander of Bomber and Attack Fighter Squadron 3E, 387th Wing Command, Luftflotte 6A!"

Max stepped back and Charles stepped forward and snapped to attention.

"I am Oberleutnant Charles Toulon, of Fighter Squadron 7A, 387th Wing Command, Luftflotte 6A!"

Charles stepped back and Hans stepped forward and snapped to attention.

"I am Oberleutnant Hans Thayer, of Fighter Squadron

7A, 387th Wing Command, Luftflotte 6A!"

Hans stepped back; the Black Knights were then marched back to Col. Kanyevev's office.

Marshal Zhukov exclaimed, "I am impressed, these men are true warriors! I can understand why the Germans did not expunge them because of their race. The Germans had everyone believing that their elite units were composed only of 'pure Aryans', what a farce!"

Commissar Khrushchev added, "I am sure the Black Knights will be of great value to us. Gen. Kartov, have them assigned to their own quarters away from the other prisoner of war officers, I will send further instructions!"

The entourage of the Supreme Commander and Commissar then left Gen. Kartov's headquarters and proceeded to their next destination.

Gen. Kartov conferred with Col. Kanyevev, "The Americans have the 'Tuskegee Airmen' to their credit, are they aware of the 'Black Knights of Germany'?"

Col. Kanyevev thought for a moment then replied, "I believe our friends in the West may want that information buried even if they knew!"

Col. Kanyevev retired to his office and informed the Black Knights, "On orders from the Supreme Commander, you Black Knights will be assigned quarters segregated from the other prisoner of war officers; consider yourselves as 'guests' of Gen. Kartov and his staff. You will also dine with us instead of your comrades."

All four Black Knights looked at each other in amazement. Otto stood up and demanded, "What is the meaning of this, what are we, guinea pigs on display? We are prisoners of war and we are to be interred with our comrades, under the terms of the Geneva Convention!"

Col. Kanyevev shouted, "I am following orders, all of you should be grateful to the Supreme Commander, HE IS SAVING YOUR LIVES!"

Col. Kanyevev then stormed from his office mumbling epithets under his breath!

Otto stated to his comrades, "I am aware that for the present this is preferential treatment but what is in store for us in the foreseeable future as soon as we have served their purpose? Beware of Russians bearing gifts!"

Max echoed Otto's reasoning, "I watched the Commissar continuously whispering to the Supreme Commander, there is more to this scenario than we suspect, we must be aware at all times and never relax our guard!"

Charles added, "I am with you Otto, you are our commanding officer!"

Hans reiterated, "All for one and one for all! That is a quote from 'The Three Musketeers'." The Black Knights then enjoyed a hearty laugh. The next day Col. Kanyevev met with Otto and they discussed the accommodations for the Black Knights. Col. Kanyevev related, "I understand your concerns for your comrades and yourself. All of you will be interrogated by our officers, your personal property, including your medals and awards, will be placed in safekeeping. There are no plans to send any of you to a prisoner of war camp at this time. Are there any questions for now? If there are any special requests then submit them to me in writing."

Otto asked, "I would like to know the fate of my commanding officer, Oberstleutnant Günter Ritter; our wingmen, Lts. Hugo von Wassel, Rolf Friedland, and Ernst Schiller; and Unteroffizier Erik Streicher, rear gunner for Hauptmann Ule. Please do that for me."

Otto thanked Col. Kanyevev and discussed the latest developments with Max, Charles and Hans.

Max stated, "I have great pessimism for the fate of my very good friend Erik, without him I would have died a thousand times."

Hans sighed, "Erik not being an officer would place him in the worst of prisoner of war camps."

Charles reassured Max, "Erik is a survivor he will make it no matter what."

Otto pondered the fate of all the young fighter pilots that were in his squadron, he did not get to know the latest replacements that arrived during the last great air battles.

A Russian guard came to the quarters of the Black Knights and announced dinner was about to be served and that he was to be their escort.

Hans said, "We are about to begin our new life in the company of our new hosts."

After refreshing themselves, the Black Knights accompanied their escort to the General's dining room. Upon entering, Gen. Kartov greeted the Black Knights; it was obvious the General had consumed many glasses of vodka.

Gen. Kartov asked, "Were the accommodations adequate for the needs of your men Hauptmann Olagande?"

Otto replied, "Everything is more than any of us expected, thank you Gen. Kartov."

Gen. Kartov continued, "I see you received the Knight's Cross of the Iron Cross for action with an infantry battalion in which you served only a few days. The commander of that battalion also received the Knights Cross with Oak Leaves and Crossed Swords, posthumously. I salute both of you. You are a brave and gallant warrior!"

Otto said, "Gen. Kartov, here is Hauptmann Max Ule, receiver of the Iron Cross 1st Grade and the Iron Cross 2nd Grade, he is one of the leading 'tank busters' in the Luftwaffe. I hate to mention it but your tank divisions met Hauptmann Ule in combat many times and he was always the victor!"

Gen. Kartov responded, "Hauptmann Ule, I salute you also, I was saving my accolades for you for last because I do know of your reputation as a 'tank buster' and I can appreciate your skills as both a Stuka pilot and an attack fighter-bomber pilot." Gen. Kartov continued, "Both of you fighter pilots, Lts. Toulon and Thayer, have over 200 confirmed air victories apiece, remarkable! I salute you Black Knights for the skills and bravery all of you exhibited over the many years of this war!"

Max stated with a chuckle, "Gentlemen, all of us here are already obsolete; the war is over and remember, history is written by the victors! Gen. Kartov, I salute you!"

The dining room resounded with loud laughter, Gen.

Kartov announced, "It is time for me to retire, enjoy your dinner." He then staggered toward the door and was assisted by two Russian soldiers who escorted him to his quarters.

Col. Kanyevev said, "The General will sleep well tonight, he was in a good mood."

In the days that followed the Black Knights were interviewed by members of the VIA (or the Vozdushnaya Istrebitelnaya Armiya, the Soviet Air Fighter Army) and interrogated by intelligence officers under the command of Maj. Aleksandr Osky. The newsreel cameras photographed the Black Knights, capturing every moment during their interviews and interrogations.

One afternoon Col. Kanyevev approached Otto after an interrogation session.

Col. Kanyevev related, "Haupt. Olagande, I have the information you asked me to obtain regarding your former commander and members of your squadron including the rear gunner, Erik Streicher."

"Thank you Col. Kanyevev, we have been very concerned about our comrades."

Otto retired to his quarters to read the reports, he called Max, Charles and Hans to join him. Included in the reports were:

> (a) Oberstleutnant Günter Ritter hospitalized at a military hospital near Moscow for treatment of congestive heart failure, condition critical.

> (b) Leutnant Hugo von Wassel interred at Prison Camp No. LN-204.

(c) Leutnant Rolf Friedland interred at Prison Camp No. LN-204.

(d) Leutnant Ernst Schiller interred at Prison Camp No. LN-204.

(e) Unteroffizier Erik Streicher interred at Prison Camp No. MGH-14.

Otto said, "They are still alive, let's hope repatriation is not long coming. According to the reports the prison camps are located in Poland, near a town called Auschwitz."

Hans stated, "I overheard part of a conversation the Russians had when discussing this town, they talked about it in a very disgusting manner, they appeared very angry and upset when they called its name."

Max said, "Let us pray for their safety."

Charles uttered, "Mein Gott! I too have heard unbelievable rumors about this town, I hope none of the rumors are true."

The four men became silent, a heavy pall of gloom and depression descended into the room.

Chapter

XVIII

The Proposition

Col. Kanyevev summoned Otto to his office, the Colonel explained, "Hauptmann Olagande, you and your men are to be transported to Moscow at once, all of you will leave your uniforms here and be given wardrobes of civilian dress, I do not know any further details at this time. Notify your men."

Otto returned to his quarters and related the latest turn of events to his comrades, "Gentlemen, we will now learn what all this 'good treatment' we have received these past months was all about, we are about to receive our new uniforms, CIVILIAN DRESS!"

"WHAT?" Hans, Charles, and Max echoed!

Otto reiterated, "Yes, we are to travel incognito until we reach Moscow."

The Black Knights were taken to a small airfield where they boarded a military transport plane.

Col. Kanyevev bided the Black Knights, "Auf Wiedersehn!", and the plane took off, destination Moscow!

After landing, a military convoy drove the Black knights to a small government building near the Kremlin. They were ushered to a large conference room and shown where they were to be seated.

A short stocky built man dressed in a dark suit entered the room followed by two military officers. The officers stood at attention until this man took his seat across the table from the Black Knights. One of the officers announced, "I am Maj. Josef Tremirov, Military Attaché to the Commissar, the other officer is Maj. Aleksandr Osky, Military Intelligence, I believe you have met him before, and this is the Commissar, Nikita Khrushchev."

The Black Knights rose from their seats to acknowledge his presence, the Commissar told them, "Be seated!" He continued, "Gentlemen, originally all of you were destined to be interred in a prisoner-of- war camp, however my staff and I have meticulously examined your records and the decision to bring the four of you here was unanimously agreed upon. The needs of my country are my first consideration. I believe, as well as the Premier, that the four of you could be of great service to the Soviet Union."

After a pause Commissar Khrushchev rose from his seat and walked around the room, the Black Knights sat rigidly in their seats wondering what the next profound statement would be as their fate was being decided!

The Commissar returned to his seat and said, "Hauptmann Ule, your academic background in engineering before you became a pilot and the success you had as a Luftwaffe pilot in destroying tanks and armored vehicles, not to mention the sinking of a British destroyer during the campaign in Norway, was brought to my attention. I was surprised that you did not receive the praise and admiration like that of your colleague, Hans-Ulrich Rudel, the famous Stuka pilot who destroyed so many of our tanks and other vehicles, now that I have met you, I fully understand!"

Commissar Khrushchev then turned toward Otto and said, "Hauptmann Olagande, you and Oberlts. Toulon and Thayer can also be of great value to the Soviet Union! Your skills as fighter pilots, fighting on all fronts against the British Royal Air Force as well as our Heroes on the Eastern Front, and attaining over 200 confirmed kills each, it is amazing!"

Commissar Khrushchev continued, "If the four of you are willing to contribute your skills and knowledge to the building of our forces of the future you will find it very rewarding.

On another note, I have some interesting news for all of you, I find it humorous, and I hope all of you can also see the ironic humor in what I am about to tell you! When the facts of your existence were presented to our 'friends in the West', The United States of America, Great Britain, and France, they denounced the facts as if they were some sort of propaganda trick. They refused to believe that there were any Luftwaffe pilots of African origin, that it was impossible! The French acknowledged that it was possible but they too were skeptical of your accomplishments, as you four have demonstrated over the course of the war. In other words, as far as our 'friends in the West' are concerned, you four men do not exist!"

The Commissar then roared in laughter! Commissar Khrushchev declared, "I have the authority to commute your 'prisoner-of-war' status and incorporate the four of you in our extensive building of our future forces. I hope all of you agree with me."

The Commissar concluded, "I will leave the room now, you Black Knights have 10 minutes to decide your fate!"

Otto looked at his comrades in silence. After a few minutes Otto said, "Let me see a show of hands, do we continue to live or do we die in some desolate gulag? We have heard rumors that the West is recruiting our best scientists and technicians, some of our best pilots are already training in the United States and Great Britain! Wing Commander Hans-Ulrich Rudel is already cooperating with the British."

Max stated, "I raise my hand in agreement to the Commissar's proposal!"

Charles and Hans raised their hands in agreement.

When the Commissar returned, Otto told him, "We Black Knights unanimously agree to your proposal!"

The Commissar stated, "Your assignments begin immediately, each of you will receive your orders before you leave this room, my aides, Maj. Tremirov and Maj. Osky, will brief you."

Chapter

XIX

The Next Leap Into the Future

The MiG-15 Jet Fighter being flown by a North Korean pilot during training exercises, circa 1949-50.

The Commissar then left the room. The Black Knights conferred with the Russian officers over their new orders, the details to be explained later.

Maj. Tremirov stated, "I am also the Liaison Officer, I will arrange your itinerary from this moment on. One of my officers will show you to your quarters located in this building, I must add that your movements are restricted, we will talk tomorrow."

The next morning the Black Knights arrived at the office of Maj. Tremirov. Maj. Tremirov was a tall man, thin but wiry. He sported a large mustache and was constantly puffing on his pipe. Maj. Osky was by contrast short and stocky, clean shaven and always carrying his swagger stick, using it to make emphatic points whenever he spoke.

Maj. Tremirov suggested, "I know of a quaint restaurant not too far from here, let us have breakfast."

The Black Knights unanimously agreed.

After dining, Maj. Tremirov took the Black Knights on a tour of the city of Moscow. Each one of them observed the sights of the city in silence, memories of the futile attempt to reach Moscow only a few years before reminded them of the tremendous cost in lives lost and the horrific conditions of the battles fought. While Maj. Tremirov was conducting the tour with these former adversaries, he too remembered when, as a young infantry officer, he and his comrades-in-arms battled against overwhelming odds, under the worst of conditions, the invincible Wehrmacht advancing toward Moscow. He also remembered how his comrades succeeded in staving off the advance and eventually saving his beloved capitol during that catastrophic winter of 1941!

Maj. Tremirov broke the silence, "Gentlemen, tomorrow we take the train to our next destination. I will supply the details after dinner tonight."

The Black Knights returned to the office of Maj. Osky to familiarize themselves with their new orders.

Maj. Osky explained, "You will be civilians with ranks as technicians and specialists, depending on the nature of your duties. You will be traveling with Maj. Tremirov to your next destination tomorrow, there will be more explanations during the journey."

Silently Otto thought to himself, "Thank you mother, again!"

Otto no longer had his 'tiny warrior doll' in his possession, the doll had been confiscated along with his other possessions when he was taken prisoner.

The morning came unheralded as the Black Knights, accompanied by Maj. Tremirov, boarded the train taking them to their next destination.

After the train pulled from the station Maj. Tremirov invited the Black Knights to meet him in the private car designed for holding conferences.

Maj. Tremirov explained, "This train is traveling under secret orders; we are the only passengers, other than the crew and special personnel assigned to assist us, including the chef, if the weather permits we will reach our destination in three days."

Max inquired, "What is our destination? I notice we are eastbound."

Maj. Tremirov replied, "I am not at liberty to say until we are about to arrive, everything connected with this trip is highly classified, on a 'need-to-know' basis."

Otto related, "I read my orders and found them vague with few details, I know you will supply the details when the time comes Maj. Tremirov."

Maj. Tremirov, replied, "That is correct. For the present time, gentlemen, enjoy the trip."

Hans asked, "Is there a Chess set on board?"

Maj. Tremirov said excitedly, "Why of course! I enjoy playing whenever I have the spare time. I hope to be a worthy opponent for you!"

Charles looked at Hans and said, "Ach, mein friend, I think you are in trouble." Both men laughed.

Maj. Tremirov went to a record player and picked out discs of music to play. The car became filled with music of the classics of Mozart, Tchaikovsky, Liszt, Beethoven, and Mendelssohn. Maj. Tremirov commented, "Music makes everything more relaxed and enjoyable, especially when taking a long trip."

After travelling for three days, the train went beyond the Ural Mountains and approached a vast plain. Maj. Tremirov announced, "We are coming to our final destination, gather your gear."

The train came to a stop at a clearing where a large bus was waiting. After boarding the bus, Maj. Tremirov and the Black Knights were driven to a large airfield.

Maj. Tremirov stated, "This is our new home Gentlemen,

for your information this place does not appear on any map, this airbase is top secret and we are restricted to this airbase. We are isolated here in this vast wilderness, over a hundred kilometers from the nearest town or village. Here you will receive instructions on how to fly our new jet aircraft and then you will train our flight instructors on how to fight with these new aircraft. They in turn will train our future fighter pilots to become the best fighters in the world."

Otto inquired, "Is another war on the horizon? If so, with whom?"

Maj. Tremirov laughed, "We must always be prepared, look what happened to my country in 1941 when your forces attacked us! We were totally unprepared and look at the price we had to pay!"

Max interrupted, "Otto, he does have a point."

Otto grumbled, "I do agree, however I am curious."

Maj. Tremirov explained, "After we have settled in our quarters we will see some of the jet plane prototypes in the testing area and we will go into the civilian area, you will get the chance to meet the people who are employed here. The atmosphere here is more relaxed than that of a strict military airbase, we are doing research here and exploring uncharted areas of flight, we need to be flexible and exchange ideas."

Charles expressed delight in seeing many women moving about, he asked, "What are their duties?"

Maj. Tremirov said, "Some are scientists, some are doctors, some are teachers and many are office personnel, they are very dedicated to this project of the future. Once they became aware of your arrival they have shown great interest in meeting all of you."

Hans sighed, "What a welcome relief, I have become weary of being in the company of nothing but MEN!"

Max cautioned, "We must stay focused on our mission, we must not allow ourselves to be so smitten that we fall into some trap. Remember, that desolate gulag is still somewhere waiting..."

Otto stated, "Max is right, we must always be careful, we are professionals."

Charles added, "We must also be flexible!"

After that remark, the Black Knights broke into laughter, even Maj. Tremirov chuckled. After being taken to their quarters the Black Knights refreshed themselves. They were anxious to tour their 'new home', as described by Maj. Tremirov. A staff car arrived at their quarters, driven by a very attractive woman chauffeur wearing a crisp white uniform. Maj. Tremirov was seated alongside the chauffeur, he leaned out of the window and beckoned the Black Knights to join him.

Maj. Tremirov introduced the chauffeur, "Gentlemen this is Lt. Elena Boskaya, she is our official chauffeur, she knows this base as well as the 'back of her hand'. We are on our way to one of the airfields, where the prototype jet fighters are being tested."

Lt. Elena Boskaya looked at the Black Knights demurely and smiled, "I am pleased to meet you gentlemen."

Max smiled and said, "Your German accent is flawless, did you ever live in Germany?"

"As a little girl," she replied, "I lived in Berlin with my aunt while I attended school there."

Max told her, "I was born in Berlin, which was my home."

The two smiled at each other, Otto looked at Max then leaned over to comment to Charles and Hans and in a whisper said, "I believe Max is smitten."

Charles whispered back, "So am I!"

Hans followed, "Don't forget about me, I haven't seen a woman smile like that in an eternity."

Arriving at the tarmac Maj. Tremirov said, "Let us go and take a close look at the new wave of the future, the jet fighter."

One of the test pilots approached them, Maj. Tremirov introduced him, "Gentlemen, this is Captain Yuri Vanev, one of our top aces from the Great Patriotic War, now one of our top test pilots."

Capt. Vanev extended his hand in greeting the Black Knights, "We pilots heard of you fantastic flyers, I never thought I would get to meet any of you, welcome to our 'home'."

Otto spotted a familiar plane parked on the tarmac, he exclaimed, "There is one of our 'Swallows' parked over there, a Messerschmitt 262 jet fighter!"

Capt. Vanev said, "Yes, and it still flies, I take it up whenever I can, it is a joy to fly!"

Charles and Hans inspected the different shapes of planes with their swept-back wings.

Hans said, "These birds appear to be fast as bullets, able to leave ordinary planes as if they were walking in the sky."

Charles agreed, "I am looking forward to flying these 'bullets'."

Max' attention was focused on the parked staff car containing the very attractive chauffeur in white.

Maj. Tremirov interrupted Max' deep thought and said, "We are developing a special plane that would be of interest to you, it is a jet 'Shturmovik' type plane, fully armored and carrying an array of cannon able to destroy the tanks of the future."

Max turned to Maj. Tremirov and said, "Yes that would be of interest to me, do you have any pictures or diagrams of this type of plane?"

The Major replied, "Yes we do, we will show you some of the prototypes, they are parked in another section of this huge complex."

Maj. Tremirov gathered the Black Knights together and said, "We must move on, we are expected in another area."

The Major instructed Lt. Boskaya to drive to the Conference Hall in the civilian section. Arriving on the scene the Black Knights were surprised to see a crowd of people standing in front of the building. Maj. Tremirov explained, "When everyone was informed of your arrival their curiosity in actually seeing Germans of African descent was overwhelming, especially after being told of the accomplishments all of you achieved in your combat experiences. For the exception of seeing soldiers of

African descent in the newsreels, that is the extent of their ever seeing someone of African descent."

Max reiterated, "The Commissar told us as far as some people believe, we do not exist!"

As the Major escorted the Black Knights into the Conference Hall, the crowd followed closely behind. The Black Knights were immediately escorted to the stage, after everyone took their seats Maj. Tremirov announced, "Ladies and gentlemen, I bring before you the former Luftwaffe's 'Black Knights' Ace fighter pilots. These four aviators have made history over the skies of Europe and our Motherland. They are here to help us build our air force to become the finest in the world. Their expertise cannot be overemphasized in this endeavor. They will need everyone's full cooperation to make this a reality. They will now introduce themselves."

Otto stepped forward, "I am Hauptmann Otto Olagande, former squadron commander of fighters, the 387th Fighter Wing Command, Luftflotte 6A. I have 203 confirmed air victories."

Otto stepped back and Max came forward, "I am Hauptmann Max Ule, former squadron commander of 'Stukas' and attack planes, the 387th Fighter Wing Command, Luftflotte 6A. I have personally destroyed over 400 tanks of all descriptions and many hundreds more of other motorized vehicles, in addition to over 40 victories of bombers and fighters."

Next Charles stepped forward, "I am Oberleutnant Charles Toulon, top experte of fighters in the 387th Fighter Wing Command, Luftflotte 6A, with over 230 confirmed air victories."

Finally, Hans stepped forward, "I am Oberleutnant Hans Thayer, experte of fighters, the 387th Fighter Wing Command, second only to Oberleutnant Toulon, and I achieved 219 confirmed air victories."

The audience sat silently in their seats, transfixed by the Black Knights commanding presence, their brown colored skin of different hues, from almond to dark chocolate, their piercing eyes, their facial features, unlike anything they had ever seen, and attempting to digest their accomplishments, everyone was speechless.

Maj. Tremirov walked to center stage and announced, "These gentlemen will eventually meet each and every one of you in time. We have to leave now."

The Black Knights and Maj. Tremirov were escorted to the waiting staff car and driven to their next destination, a quiet dinner.

As the winter of 1947 approached Otto noted that there were no severe weather patterns, he discussed this with his comrades, "We must be in the southern part of Russia, I know we are east of the Ural Mountains, they picked this place very carefully for their training and research facilities. The only news allowed into this facility is filtered through their top command center and, according to Maj. Tremirov, he does not have top-secret clearance so there is little he can tell me on what is happening in the outside world."

Hans said, "I notice there is a sense of urgency in completing the training of the fighter instructors ahead of the scheduled dates we were originally given."

Charles stated, "I noticed that sense of urgency too."

Max said, "The Major mentioned that I would be

transferred to another facility soon, he seemed to imply that I would be going alone. I told him that if he separated us that he could at least let my little Elena accompany me when I go to my next assignment. He promised me he would try to keep us together."

Maj. Tremirov summoned the Black Knights to his office, excitedly he said, "The fighter plane the Soviet High Command has approved of is made by the Mikoyan-Gurevich Aircraft Bureau, it will be designated the Mi-G15, armed with a 23mm cannon and two machine guns!"

Otto stated, "I knew that plane would be chosen, it handled so well, especially in tight turns, and it had superior speed to the other prototypes."

Hans added, "That plane has been the mainstay of my classes, my students are ahead in their training now that the Mi-G15 will be the main fighter!"

Charles inquired, "What other jet fighters are out there in the world, jet fighters from The United States of America and Great Britain? I sometimes wonder, we do not hear of anything concerning those countries."

Max queried, "On that note, what is happening in Germany?"

Maj. Tremirov stated, "I do get some news of what is happening in Germany, the country is being rebuilt, and the railroads are running on time. Your country has been divided into zones, the city of Berlin is in our Soviet Zone. The weather is cold and clear today, and that is the news!" The Major added, "I do not hear anything about our former allies, they are not mentioned in the news I get from the command center, which is strange. I have been advised not to be too inquisitive. I pass this advice along to all of you."

Otto mused, "A point well taken, we have enough duties to occupy 40 people as it is."

The next months approaching 1949 produced a record number of graduate aviation flight instructors. Maj. Tremirov received a communique from the central command center praising the personnel for their effort in attaining the goal, he notified the Black Knights immediately of the praise for their input.

Maj. Tremirov said, "I have been informed that there will be flight instructors from the Republic of China and the Korean Peninsula enrolled in future classes and will be supplied with translators in both Russian and German." Maj. Tremirov paused before continuing, taking a few puffs on his ever present pipe, he looked at Max and said, "Hauptmann Max Ule, you will be transferred to the Bureau of Armored Vehicles and Tanks immediately. The good news is that Lt. Elena Boskaya will also be transferred to your unit."

The Black Knights gathered around Max, embracing him and wishing him well. Otto lifted his cup of coffee and made a toast, "Here is to our Max, that he be successful in his future role and that we all meet again!"

Maj. Tremirov exclaimed, "Here, here, to a most worthy officer!"

Max raised his cup of coffee and toasted, "To my comrades and my friend, Maj. Tremirov, I cannot fully express my emotions, my gratitude in serving with you, and the lives we have lived together. I wish to express my gratitude to you, Maj. Tremirov, for arranging the transfer of my little Elena to accompany me on my next journey, you have made me very happy!"

Everyone in the room did the best they could to hide their emotions as Max retired to his quarters to gather his gear and depart.

Chapter

XX

More Surprises as
the Future Unfolds

The remaining three Black Knights continued their roles as trainers for the Oriental pilots of the Republic of China and the Korean Republic.

As the summer months of 1949 waned and the present class was about to graduate, Maj. Tremirov conferred with the Black Knights, "What is your opinion of these Oriental pilots?"

Otto replied, "They seem to be very capable pilots but a few of them seem to approach 'dog fighting' tactics undisciplined, they seem to enjoy the tricks of twisting and turning instead of controlled flight and depending on their wingman for support."

Charles added, "I also found that to be true of some of my students. When I brought that point to their attention one of them told me, 'You were once a very innovative fighter pilot, according to the reports you flew circles around your opponents!' I tried to explain to them that I took the time to develop my skills and to study and thoroughly know the peculiar characteristics of my 'mount'."

Hans concurred, "I had to discipline those pilots that could not break themselves from that bad habit."

Maj. Tremirov continued, "I hope they conform as quickly as possible, their training program has been shortened because their respective countries have issued orders for their return as soon as possible."

Otto looked at his comrades and said, "Let's get back to work!"

After another three weeks passed, the Oriental pilots were graduated and returned to their respective countries.

Maj. Tremirov summoned the Black Knights to meet him at the command center. Maj. Tremirov introduced the Black Knights to the commander of the airbase, Marshal Anatoly Alkudin.

Marshal Alkudin said, "I am pleased with the results of your invaluable training techniques that helped produce the finest flight instructors and who are now able to insure that we will have the finest fighter pilots in the world."

Marshal Alkudin continued, "You Black Knights have been ordered to return to Moscow immediately with Maj. Tremirov for further instructions. Hauptmann Max Ule has already returned to Moscow. He has also received my praise for his contributions to our efforts in producing the finest tanks in the world."

The Black Knights collectively thanked the Marshal and with Maj. Tremirov, they departed to their quarters to gather their gear and board the awaiting train to Moscow.

The Black Knights boarded the train in silence and did not utter a word until the train started moving westward. After that, they released a loud cheer!

Otto exclaimed, "I cannot believe it, after these past two years we are returning to civilization!"

Maj. Tremirov added, "I have an additional surprise for all of you, the Marshal sent a special gift to Hauptmann Ule as a token for his appreciation."

Maj. Tremirov left the car and said, "I will soon return."

Hans said, "I am speechless, whatever the future brings I am ready!"

Charles echoed, "Me too!"

Maj. Tremirov returned, "Gentlemen, I have returned with the special gift to Hauptmann Ule, I present LT. ELENA BOSKAYA, the finest and prettiest chauffeur in all of Russia!" Again, the Black Knights let out a loud cheer!

Lt. Elena Boskaya said, "This is all such a pleasant surprise, I thought I had lost Max forever!"

Hans reassured her, "When Max sees you he will faint with joy!"

Otto looked at his comrades and repeated, "I cannot believe it, all of this is some kind of miracle!"

Charles stated, "Almighty God is great, we must pray for his strength and guidance as the future unfolds!"

Maj. Tremirov said nothing but on close observation, the Major was seen making the sign of the Cross in the reverse order, the custom as practiced in the Russian Orthodox Church.

Music was piped throughout the train as it made its way toward Moscow. For the next three days, everyone was in a joyous mood while awaiting his or her fate.

A convoy of five cars, consisting of one limousine, met the train as it pulled into a remote section of the Moscow Station that was under heavy guard.

Maj. Aleksandr Osky exited the limousine and

instructed Maj. Tremirov, Lt. Boskaya, and the three Black Knights to enter the limo and make themselves comfortable. The convoy immediately drove from the station with sirens blaring!

Maj. Osky told the group, "There have been some disagreements with our former allies since you have been gone and the situation has become somewhat tense. When we arrive at Commissar Khrushchev's headquarters he will explain everything."

As soon as they arrived the group was ushered into the conference room, Maj. Osky directed them to their seats. After a wait of 10 minutes the Commissar walked in, everyone rose to attention.

He ordered, "Be seated! You may have noticed there are armed sentries everywhere, just a precaution, tight security! Our former allies have partitioned Germany into zones; they also did the same thing in Berlin. In order to unify Berlin the city was sealed off from our 'friends in the West'. They countered with an airlift that was just lifted before your arrival."

The Commissar continued, "I have issued orders repatriating all of you Black Knights, you will be allowed to return to your homes, you have been of great service to my country. The Premier sends his thanks for a job well done, I also wish to add my appreciation of gratitude."

The Commissar ordered Maj. Osky to have Hauptmann Max Ule brought forward and for Maj. Tremirov and Lt. Boskaya to have seats in another office until they were sent for.

When Max entered the conference room and saw his fellow comrades, he was overcome with joy at the unexpected surprise!

The Commissar told Max, "I have just informed your comrades that all of you have been repatriated and are free to return to your homes. I understand that your home is in Berlin, in the zone controlled by The United States of America."

The Commissar looked at Otto and said, "Your home is in Africa, if you wish to return to your homeland I will arrange for your transportation."

The Commissar then addressed Charles and Hans, "Your homes are in the American Zone, there will be no trouble in your relocating to your respective homes."

The Commissar ordered, "Maj. Osky, bring Maj. Tremirov and the special guest here at once!"

"Yes Sir!" Maj. Osky replied.

Maj. Osky returned with Maj. Tremirov and Lt. Boskaya, Max stood transfixed, unable to say a word as Elena entered the room!

The Commissar said, "I will leave now, your documents are being prepared, you will be able to leave for your destinations within the hour!"

After the Commissar left the room the Black Knights rushed to embrace each other, Max yelled, "Halt!" He then embraced his 'little Elena' and told the others, "She comes first!" Lt. Elena Boskaya was a very happy woman indeed!

Otto told Maj. Tremirov, "We will never forget you, on behalf of my comrades, you are truly the best friend anyone could have under these circumstances. You will always be welcome in my home and my heart!"

Charles and Hans echoed the same sentiment, "You are our friend forever! Who would have ever believed that this could happen?"

Max and Elena retired to the privacy of the other office; Max and Elena were crying in each other's arms, they were shedding tears of joy.

Max recovered enough to ask Elena, "Will you marry me, I have never known true love before, I realize now that there is no future for me without you."

Elena replied, "Yes I will, this is the happiest moment of my life, if my life ended at this moment I would be able to say, I have truly lived if only for a moment!"

The documents for the Black Knights were delivered.

Maj. Osky announced, "You are all free to go, I have been given instructions to arrange accommodations for all of you to have transportation to your chosen destinations."

Maj. Osky and Maj. Tremirov shook hands and exchanged glances of approval at the sight that unfolded before their eyes, there were no words uttered.

Max and Elena composed themselves and emerged from the other office. Together they announced their engagement.

Maj. Osky also announced, "I authorize that Lt. Elena Boskaya be given 60 days extended furlough and her pass will allow her to go anywhere she desires!"

Max stated, "We are off to Berlin, Elena must meet my parents! Immediately after that, we are going to be married! I wish for all of you to attend our wedding, especially you Maj. Tremirov, without you I may never have met Elena!"

Otto said, "Maj. Osky, Berlin is our destination, book us at the Hotel Continental!"

Maj. Osky said, "Before all of you leave I would like to give you this sealed box to accompany you on your journey, you can open it when you book into the Hotel Continental. I wish all of you 'Auf Wiedersehn' and to you Lt. Boskaya, I wish you and Max all the happiness possible in your future life."

Chapter

XXI

For Max Ule, Another Beginning,
It is a Wonderful Life

After arriving in Berlin the Black Knights and Maj. Tremirov, checked into the Hotel Continental, Max reserved the bridal suite for himself and Elena.

Max said, "Now to find my parents, Berlin has gone through a huge transformation with all the reconstruction, I doubt if I would recognize my old neighborhood. Otto, come along with me, I am going to hire a taxicab."

Max then asked Charles and Hans to arrange the wedding; if the church was not available then they would be married in the main conference hall of the hotel.

Max directed the taxi driver to his old neighborhood. They observed many new apartment buildings in different stages of construction along the main thoroughfare.

Otto commented, "This is a huge city, this is my first time being here."

Max told the driver, "Slow down, I think this is the street that my house was located on. I am going to get out and walk around, follow me."

Max walked to a young couple seated on a bench and inquired, "Do you know a family named Ule that I believe lived in this neighborhood?"

The young man replied, "There are a man and his wife, an interracial couple about the age of 50 that live on the second floor of that apartment building across the street. Their name is Ule. My wife and I live on the first floor."

Max thanked the couple, ran back to the taxi, and excitedly exclaimed, "Come Otto, I found them!"

Max and Otto walked to the door and rang the bell, a deep voice inside inquired, "Who is there?"

Max hollered excitedly, "It is Max!"

The door opened and there stood a tall stocky man, with very dark skin and the classic etched features of a Zulu warrior, staring at Max and Otto in disbelief!

The man called to his wife, "Olga, come here quickly, our son has come home! Max is here!"

Max' mother enveloped him within her arms and she said repeatedly, "Max you are home, safe and sound, I am so happy!"

After the tearful reunion, Max introduced his friend and comrade, Otto, to his parents.

Max excitedly said, "Mother, father, Otto and I are staying at the Hotel Continental, both of you have to come now. I am getting married and I want both of you to meet your new daughter!"

Stunned, Shaka Ule expressed his delight, "The world is changing so fast! Olga, help me catch up to the present, we have our son back and now he speaks of our acquiring a daughter too, what is this world coming to?"

Otto stepped outside and summoned the taxi to take everyone back to the hotel. Arriving at the hotel Hans rushed to Max and informed him the wedding would take place in the hotel conference hall and that a priest was available.

Max brought his parents in and introduced them to Charles, Hans and Maj. Tremirov. He then asked, "Where is Elena?"

Charles said, "Elena is in the bridal suite resting, maybe you should tell her you found your parents and

the wedding will be held in the hotel conference hall this evening."

Max said, "Things are happening so fast, I never had these problems when I was in the thick of battle! I need help!"

Otto calmed Max, "We are here with you, no need to worry!"

Max then went to the bridal suite to tell Elena all the events that had transpired.

Elena told Max tearfully, "I am so happy your parents are here, I wish mine were here too."

Max reassured her that they would visit her parents during their honeymoon.

The hotel staff hurriedly prepared for the gala event, one of the staff went to Elena and offered her assistance in obtaining a wedding dress. Elena was so surprised but the young woman assured her, "We do this all the time! We are prepared for all emergencies, which is why we are the finest hotel in Europe!"

Other guests at the hotel consisted of military personnel of high rank from America, Russia, France and Great Britain, political figures, captains of industry, and wealthy tourists. There was a rash of conversation among them as to who these four men, of dark hue, were and what was their connection to an officer of the Russian Red Army. They all wondered what was their source of power that could command the entire hotel staff to do their every bidding, including having a small and private, but lavish, wedding performed in the hotel conference hall! The main topic among the guests was,

'Who was invited?' or 'Who was NOT invited?' One of the members of the Soviet military brass received a discreet telephone call 'advising' all Russian personnel to cease making inquiries at once! The Russians, of all stripes, retired from the scene in haste! An American reporter that was in the lobby to cover another story noticed this strange behavior and attempted to read the hotel registry but found no names were registered, the registry was blank! The mystery deepened. The hotel security forbade anyone to approach the four men of dark hue and their entourage during their stay at the hotel.

Max told his parents, "Don't be concerned about the tight security, we are use to it. You will have comfortable seats in the conference hall, I want both of you to relax and enjoy yourselves."

Elena informed Max that she was almost ready; the Black Knights and Max' parents entered the conference hall followed by Maj. Tremirov and the priest. The doors to the hall were then closed to the public.

The ceremony was performed with elegance, a sumptuous dinner followed. Now as man and wife, the couple embraced and bid everyone 'Au Revoir' as they retired to the bridal suite. Shaka Ule sat next to Otto and said, "Both Olga and I are in a state of shock, for years we heard little from Max, we did not know what locations he was writing from and nothing of what he was doing. We are very grateful he has returned.

You men refer to yourselves as 'The Black Knights', we would hear of the exploits of the 'Black Knights' in the newsreels and magazines, are you and your men and our Max really the same 'Black Knights'?"

Otto said, "Yes Sir, we are the ones, but I do not know

what was being said, we just did our job."

Otto continued, "You parents have every reason to be proud of Max, he has been a hero time and time again, he has attained records that equaled the best of any warrior that ever went into battle. He is the receiver of the Iron Cross more than once and was about to receive the Knight's Cross to the Iron Cross. The War ended before that could happen."

Maj. Tremirov came over to join in the conversation.

"There is a sealed box upstairs in your room, Otto. I want you to take Max' parents upstairs and in the presence of all of us I want you to open it." Everyone retired to Otto's room.

Otto placed the sealed box on his bed and proceeded to open it, everyone gathered closely as the wrappings were being removed. When Otto opened the box he gasped, "Our medals and awards have been returned, my tiny warrior doll is here also! Hans, Charles, here are our logs!"
"

"Herr Ule, here are Max' awards, medals, and his official logs. This is living proof of his accomplishments!"

Otto continued, "These records are the real story of the Black Knights!"

Maj. Tremirov added, "There is more to the saga of the Black Knights but the cloak of secrecy will cloud that story for the time being, however I will add it is worth the admiration of their deeds for all time!"

Frau Ule said, "I am so proud of Max." She then burst into tears. Herr Ule put his arms around her and said,

"We are all proud of Max and we are also proud of you Black Knights!"

Herr Ule said, "Gentlemen, I believe it is time for mama and I to go home and retire, this has been a wonderful day and we have been blessed. We will be here tomorrow to send Elena and Max off on their honeymoon."

Otto said, "I will summon a taxi and ride with you."

After depositing Herr and Frau Ule at their door, Otto returned to the hotel.

Everyone arose early the next morning. Max' parents returned to the hotel and met Otto who escorted them to the dining room where they joined Hans, Charles and Maj. Tremirov who were already engaged in having their breakfast.

"Where are the bride and groom?" "Are they ever going to awaken?" The questions came in flurries as everyone awaited their presence.

Elena and Max finally appeared. They were greeted with a chorus of "Join us!" As everyone rose from their seats to make way for them as they took their place at the head of the table. Max announced, "When we leave here we will be on our way to the Black Sea resort city of Odessa where we are to meet Elena's parents!"

Congratulations came from the many guests in the dining room as Elena and Max acknowledged all those present. After dining with their friends and Max' parents they were escorted to a waiting limousine to drive them to their train. The Hotel Concierge presented Elena with a large bouquet of roses before she entered the limousine.

Maj. Tremirov told the Black Knights, "Gentlemen, I have received orders for me to return to the Kremlin immediately. I hope we meet again someday, working with all of you these past years have been a very enlightening and enjoyable experience, I bid you Auf Wiedersehn!"

After Maj. Tremirov departed, the Black Knights gathered in Otto's room to decide on their next course of action.

Charles said, "I am going to my home in Saarbrucken, my parents own a small café there. During my school years I learned to bake, I brought little cakes to school for my classmates. I wish to cleanse my mind of the war years and become 'human' again."

Hans replied, "I am going to my home in Neundettelsau, it was a small farming town when I was growing up, not too far from Nuremburg. I too wish to forget."

Otto related, "And I will go to my home in Cameroon, Africa. I am considered one of the Elders of my tribe, the Ubo, I will be glad to see my mother again and learn the history of my tribal roots."

Charles said, "No matter which roads our lives take, we must never lose contact with one another."

Hans quoted from the 'Three Musketeers', "All for one and one for all!"

Otto announced, "If for any reason we must meet again, the Hotel Continental here in Berlin will be our meeting place."

The Black Knights arranged for their respective destinations then departed.

Chapter

XXII

Otto Olagande Making a Return
Journey to Mother Africa

Otto's plane landed at the city of Douala, Cameroon. Otto hired a car and driver to take him inland to the territory occupied by the Ubo tribe. The beauty of the country fascinated Otto as the car traveled the winding roads into the interior. After traveling for two days, the car approached a large stately house that looked familiar to him.

Otto told the driver, "I used to live in that house, pull up to the entrance."

The driver looked at Otto in awe and said, "That is the home of Queen Tikwana Olagande, now I see the resemblance, you must be her son!"

Otto replied, "That is correct, I am her son."

Security officers instantly surrounded the car; one of the officers approached and inquired, "What business do you have here?"

Otto replied, "I am Otto Olagande, son of Queen Tikwana Olagande. Please inform the Queen that her son, Otto, has returned home."

The officer sent one of his men inside the house with the message. After a few minutes the officer returned and informed his superior, "The Queen ordered that he be brought to her immediately!"

Otto was escorted to the main study hall of the house. The Queen, a tall stately woman, with graying hair, wearing the ceremonial robes of nobility, surrounded by uniform security officers and her Chief of Staff, appeared. Her large brown eyes staring intensely at the man standing before her, she gasped, "It is true, my son Otto has returned!"

Queen Tikwana reached out to Otto; Otto stepped forward and embraced her, he held her tightly in his arms and sobbed, "I dreamt of this moment countless times, never believing I would actually live to see this!"

Moments of silence passed as mother and son embraced. The Queen wiped her eyes and ordered, "See to it that the other Elders are notified of my son's return, there will be a feast tonight! Take his driver to the guest house and see to his needs and make him comfortable!"

The Queen instructed her Chief of Staff to have Otto assigned to quarters reserved for diplomatic guests. She looked at Otto and said, "We can talk later, now you must rest!"

That evening a feast was prepared; all the Elders attended. Otto sat next to his great-uncle, Chief Umgato Olagande.

Chief Umgato whispered to Otto, "You must tell us of your adventures, we received many communiqués from time to time of the Great War that enveloped the European continent." After the festivities subsided, Chief Umgato instructed the Elders to retire to the council room, he told Otto, "You are to be introduced, walk with me."

Chief Umgato announced, "Elders, this is Otto Olagande, son of Queen Tikwana, and grandson of our most beloved chief, King Nkuno Olagande, who died recently. Otto now holds the title of Honorary Elder as bequeathed by our laws concerning the heirs of chiefs."

Chief Umgato continued, "Elder Otto Olagande has returned from distant lands where he fought in many battles in the tradition of a great warrior and emerged victorious! He fought for the nation of Germany, the country of his father, and received many honors and awards for his many heroic deeds."

Chief Umgato motioned for Otto to stand before the Elders and continue with the introduction.

Otto announced to the Elders, "My great-uncle, Chief Umgato, has honored me in presenting me to all of you. I was a captain in the Luftwaffe; I held the rank of Hauptmann, squadron commander of fighters, 387th Fighter Wing. I fought against the British, the French, and the Russians across the European continent, the Mediterranean, the Balkans, and the Eastern Front of Russia! It is a miracle that I am standing here, alive and well!"

The Elders listened in silence and awe as Otto described himself, when Otto finished one of the Elders announced, "We are proud to have one of our members become a warrior of such distinction as you, Elder Otto."

Otto confided to Chief Umgato that he be excused, he said, "I wish to see my mother now and I am so tired."

The Chief had Otto transported to Queen Tikwana's quarters. The Queen was standing at the entrance when Otto arrived.

"Mother, I have been presented before the Elders by Chief Umgato and was well received, but I had to come to you and thank you for saving my life repeatedly. I carried the tiny 'warrior doll' you gave me whenever I went into combat and I survived, every time! Mother, I am giving you this case, it contains all of my medals, decorations, and citations. If it were not for your prayers and the 'warrior doll' I would not be alive today!"

Queen Tikwana smiled, "I did pray every night for your safety and having you here standing before me is living proof I have been amply rewarded. I hope you will stay and be part of the governing body of our tribe. We are an important integral part of the central government, our people are well educated and our tribe is prosperous because of the many rich deposits of minerals we have on our land."

Otto hesitantly answered, "The country is very beautiful and peaceful my mother, after I have spent some time reacquainting myself with my surroundings I will give you my answer."

Otto then retired to his quarters.

As the summer of 1950 approached, Otto found himself in the role as a mediator in inter-tribal affairs as he sat at the council table with the other Elders. On occasion Otto would be part of a welcoming committee for the arrival of other tribal chiefs visiting on state functions, sitting with Chief Umgato and Queen Tikwana as they received their guests.

On 25 June, Otto received news of the beginning of a civil war on the Asian peninsula of Korea. This fateful news was about to change the course of the lives of the Black Knights.

Otto thought, "So that was the reason for the hasty return of the Oriental flight instructors and pilots to their homeland, they were preparing for war!"

Otto requested an immediate audience with his mother and Chief Umgato.

Otto explained, "There is a civil war in progress on the

Korean Peninsula, I must return to Berlin at once and contact my fellow comrades. I cannot explain now, the future is uncertain for me and I cannot fully commit to my role as an Elder, at least not at this time. I beg your forgiveness my mother, I know you had hopes that I could assimilate back to my tribal roots and live the rest of my life in these peaceful surroundings, maybe at a later date but not for now!"

Queen Tikwana said, "Go my son, I understand and I will again pray for your safe return. Speaking as your mother, I want you to stay, but as the Queen, I know you must fulfill your destiny, my warrior son."

Mother and son embraced as she sobbed uncontrollably.

Chief Umgato added, "I understand the spirit of a true warrior, which is a great part of you, may the Gods watch over you!"

Otto then departed.

After Queen Tikwana regained her composure, she turned to her uncle, Chief Umgato, and lamented, "My son's European culture is more prominent within him than his African culture."

The Chief nodded silently in agreement.

Chapter

XXIII

A Long Awaited Visit Home
for Charles Toulon

Charles wired his parents ahead of his arrival that he was alive and safe and within two days would be on his way home. Greta and François Toulon, Charles' parents announced to all the patrons of their café that their son was coming home and preparations would be made for the welcoming ceremonies.

Charles' father arrived at the train station early and had a delegation of well-wishers, including a small band, with him. As the train pulled into the station, the band started playing 'Auld Lang Syne'. The train pulled to a halt and Charles emerged, his father rushed to him and the two embraced.

Charles said, "It has been a long time…"

His father interrupted, "You do not have to say anything, you are home! Your mother is anxiously waiting, come!"

Charles waved to the crowd as he entered his father's car, soon everyone was on their way to the café.

Standing at the café entrance was his mother, Charles exited the car and rushed to her, the two embraced as she repeated again and again, "Danke Mein Gott, Danke!"

The crowded café erupted in cheers! "Charles is home! Charles is home!" The band played festive music and folk songs welcoming their 'Hero'. The celebration continued into the late hours of the night.

A very tired Charles told his parents, "I am ready to retire, is my old bedroom still available?"

His mother reassured him, "No one has been in your room since you left many years ago."

Charles bid the crowd, "Gute Nacht, one and all!" He then left for his home and retired.

The next day Charles inquired as to the state of the family business, his father stated the café was doing well and that he was thinking of expanding.

Charles said, "Father, I have been dreaming of owning a bakery ever since I was a boy, I am going to make inquiries and perhaps open a bakery here in Saarbrucken."

His father exclaimed, "Wonderful! I remember when you baked little cakes as a boy and took them to school. Your mother will be very happy of your decision."

As the months of 1950 progressed, Charles found a location for his bakery and he started making plans for its construction. On 25 June, one of his neighbors came to him with a newspaper that had a major story of a civil war that began on the Korean Peninsula and that the war involved the United States of America! Charles stared at the newspaper in disbelief! Charles was speechless as he read the article repeatedly! When Charles approached his father with the newspaper, his father said, "That war is in Asia, many thousands of kilometers from here, it does not involve us, continue with your plans for your bakery!"

Charles said, "Father, I must contact my former commander, Otto Olagande, there is much that I cannot discuss with you and mother at this time. The last I heard from him he was at his home in Cameroon, Africa."

Charles' father exclaimed, "How ironic, a telegram arrived for you earlier this day from Herr Olagande, in the telegram he stated for you to meet him in Berlin immediately!"

Charles stated, "I don't know how to approach mother with my hasty departure, please handle that for me, I will explain everything at a later time. I authorize you to continue with my plans concerning the bakery. I hope to return soon."

Charles then departed to Berlin.

Chapter

XXIV

The Surprise Visit Home
for Hans Thayer

Hans returned to his home in Neundettelsau, a farming town. He hired a taxi to drive him from the train station to his parent's home; he was laden with presents for his mother and a gift of a carved pipe for his father. Hans had not notified his parents of his coming home as he elected to surprise them.

Hans' father was in the field driving a tractor when he saw the taxi pulling up to the house. Hans' mother was inside cooking.

Hans rang the bell and knocked on the door. Hans' mother opened the door and shrieked, "Hans, it is you! You have come home!" She went outside and beckoned Hans' father to come quickly. Karl Thayer turned his tractor toward the house and drove up to the front door. He looked at the tall bronze man standing there smiling at him, "Hans, my son! I cannot believe it, you have come home!"

Hans hugged both of his parents and said, "Mother, father, I am so happy to see you and that both of you survived the war! Whenever I had a private moment I worried about both of you!"

His mother replied, "We have been worrying about you ever since you left to join the Luftwaffe, up until this very moment!"

Hans said, "The farm looks so much larger, I see you have farm helpers out in the wheat field."

His father said, "Yes those are immigrants from Turkey, they are a great help. They come from a pool of helpers housed in the poorer section of town. I hope that you will join your mother and me in the operation of the farm."

Hans replied, "Father, I have applied for a position as a pilot with the Lufthansa Air Line, I am awaiting their call. Flying is in my blood, I miss living in the sky!"

"Come inside my son, I have cooked cabbage and beef, you need to grace the family table." Marie and Karl Thayer beamed with pride as their son hugged them as they entered the house. Hans said, "I will stay for a while, it is so good to get away from it all, to rest up from the fast life. I will be of whatever help I can for now."

"You must tell us all about your war experiences my son, we are so thankful you are home safe and sound." His father said.

The months passed slowly in 1950 as summer approached. Hans was idly listening to the radio on 25 June when he heard the announcer say, "Korean troops from the north have invaded the southern peninsula controlled by the Republic of Korea, they have attacked the garrisons of American troops stationed there. A civil war has started!"

Hans summoned his parents and announced, "I must contact my former commanding officer, Otto Olagande, he went to his home in Cameroon, Africa, at the same time I came here. There may be ramifications for the peace as to the events that are occurring on the other side of the world!"

"What has that got to do with you, my son?" both parents asked.

Hans replied, "I did not tell you much about my war experiences and my role after the war, and hopefully my military service has ended. I must return to Berlin at once, my future will be decided there."

Hans prepared for his return to Berlin; there was a tearful farewell for the Thayer family as Hans summoned a taxi to take him to the train station.

After Hans departed, his father caressed his mother as she cried and said, "We have gone through this before, my Marie, Hans will be alright, he is a survivor!"

Chapter

XXV

A Shocking News Event and
the Black Knights are Reunited

Max and Elena returned to Berlin after their honeymoon, they settled in the countryside suburb of Kreuzberg. Max enjoyed his position as a designer in the engineering department of a subsidiary of the Krupp Heavy Industries.

The spring of 1950 saw little change in the political climate in Berlin. One day Max had a surprise visitor at his office, Col. Josef Tremirov!

Max greeted him, "What a pleasant surprise, I see you have been promoted, let us go to the cafeteria for coffee."

Col. Tremirov replied, "I do not have much time, I had to see you, an old friend, while I was here in Berlin on official business."

The Colonel continued, "Max, soon there will be a series of events that will change the politics of the major nations of the world. You and your comrades, the Black Knights, were on a highly classified mission during the year, 1947, when we traveled to the far eastern part of southern Russia, beyond the Ural Mountains. Although your contributions enabled my government to evaluate and judge its place as a present day super power, the four of you were but an infinitesimal part of the total picture."

Max queried, "I am afraid I do not understand. What are you trying to tell me?"

Col. Tremirov continued, "The Americans are developing new and sophisticated weapons, their aircraft industry is experimenting with futuristic fighters and bombers to carry their atomic weapons. These weapons must be tested under battlefield conditions but not at the risk of going to war! We must know our capabilities if we ever have to face these weapons!"

Max asked, "Do you mean there will be future 'Wars by Proxy', wars that will not directly involve the super powers against one another?"

The Colonel continued, "Max, you are a very intelligent and observant individual, soon you will hear of events that may startle your comrades and temporarily disrupt their lives but they are not to be concerned, they will NOT be affected. I can only imagine that your former commander, Otto Olagande, may feel compelled to gather all of you together for an important mission but that will not be necessary! It will be up to you to calm their fears. We have our own personnel in place to give us the necessary answers to whatever problems that may emerge."

Max said, "I understand, you are truly a friend."

After Col. Tremirov left, Max called his secretary to cancel his business appointments for the rest of the day.

Max went home and told Elena, "We will soon have guests, my comrades will be coming to Berlin."

Elena asked, "When?"

Max answered, "Very soon!"

Spring turned into summer, on 25 June 1950, news of a civil war on the Korean Peninsula brought a shock to the world!

Max thought deeply about the news and sighed, "Yes, we can expect guests very soon!"

Otto arrived in Berlin and checked in at the Hotel Continental; soon Charles and Hans, who arrived shortly thereafter, joined him. Otto had a message waiting for him at the hotel desk, the manager presented it to him. Otto read the message and it said, "Welcome from your comrade and friend, Max, expect me for dinner."

Otto gathered Charles and Hans to his suite and told them, "We are to have dinner with Max, there are important things to discuss!"

The hotel provided a private dining room for Otto and his guests. Max was already seated in the room when Otto, Charles and Hans arrived.

Max announced, "Gentlemen, I am here on a mission, to inform all of you that none of us will be involved in any way with this 'War by Proxy' that is in progress on the Korean Peninsula."

Otto said, "I had the fear that we would be called to participate in the air war but you are here to tell us that those fears are ungrounded, is that true?"

Max stated, "That is true, the Russians are using their own pilots, integrated with the North Korean pilots, to test their own skills against the skills of the Americans."

Charles exclaimed, "What a way for us to have an unscheduled reunion!"

Max continued, "A very good friend of ours paid me a visit during the spring to warn me of the events we are now witnessing. Now that you know the truth you can all return to your homes."

Hans said, "I am here on business anyway, I am to be offered a pilot's position with Lufthansa Airlines.

Charles said, "I can get back to my bakery, the plans are already drawn up. I want all of you there when I open the doors for business."

Otto related, "Although I am relieved that I can get on with my life, I am not going back to Cameroon at this time, I am going to pursue my dream of producing music productions and plays."

Max, Charles and Hans looked at Otto in stunned silence. After a moment of silence they chorused, "What? A music producer? A producer of plays?"

Max exclaimed, "I have never heard you say anything about producing plays or music productions, this must be a joke or some fantasy!"

Otto said, "The 'fantasy' came to me as I fought the Russians during the Battle of Kursk. We came together as if we were all part of a great orchestra or a great opera company and I was the conductor. It may sound crazy but I intend to see it through! I am going to stay here in Berlin, perhaps in a small apartment in the section of Berlin where the avant garde artists live."

Hans laughed, "They are all starving there!"

Otto retorted, "All of you seem to forget, I receive an ample stipend regularly, enough to indulge in my fantasies, without the threat of 'starving'."

Max said, "Otto is right, I wish him all the success of his dreams."

Hans said, "I am not returning home either, my parents are very sad, but I have to fly, that is now and has always been my dream!"

Charles added, "My dream, other than flying, was to become a baker. My bakery is already under construction; my father has it on hold until I return. I will wire my parents of my return, I know they will be overjoyed!"

Max stated, "I am living my dream now, I am an engineer and designer at the Krupp Heavy Industries Conglomerate and I have a comfortable home in Kreuzberg with my beloved Elena, who is no longer in the army I might add! I am very thankful that we live in close proximity to my parents' apartment."

Otto lamented, "I left a grieving Queen, my mother, and a sad great-uncle, the chief of my tribe, with little or no explanation about my hasty departure, I must make amends. I will compose a lengthy letter begging for forgiveness."

The Black Knights further discussed their plans and after completing their dinner retired to their suites, Max drove back home.

The next morning Charles took an early train back to Saarbrucken, he eagerly anticipated seeing his parents again and completing the construction of his bakery.

Hans received a telephone call from the personnel manager of Lufthansa Airlines requesting that he come for an interview as early as possible.

Otto arose early and hired a taxi to take him on a tour of the avant garde artists' district in Berlin. Otto mused, "The look on the faces of my comrades when I told them of my dreams and aspirations was priceless, I will never forget their expressions to my dying day!" Otto then laughed aloud!

Max had an early breakfast and told Elena, "Our reunion went quite well and the dinner was great, I am pleased to say our lives are back on track."

Max then drove to his office. A visitor was waiting for his arrival, Col. Tremirov! Max and Col. Tremirov greeted each other warmly with the customary 'bear hug'.

Max exclaimed, "Glad to see you my friend, my comrades did as you had predicted but I reassured them they could continue with their lives and not attach any importance to the events occurring in Asia as far as their personal lives were concerned."

Col. Tremirov replied, "Now I can really appreciate why the Luftwaffe High Command held Otto Olagande in such high esteem as a leader! Please give him my personal regards, I must return immediately to Moscow! I would love to stay and have a cup of coffee with you but duty calls!"

After the Colonel left Max' office, Max had his secretary notify Otto and Hans to meet him and Elena at his home for dinner. Max called home and told Elena of his plans for the dinner.

Otto continued on his tour until he noticed a small coffee house located on a side street that appeared abandoned, he ordered the driver to pull over then exited the taxi. On closer examination, the coffee house was not abandoned, inside Otto observed a young man sweeping the premises. Otto inquired as to the ownership of the establishment. The young man answered, "I am the owner, this place was owned by my parents before they were killed in an air raid during the War but now it is mine."

Otto asked, "How is business?"

The young man laughed, "As you can see, an occasional customer may stroll in but for the most part, I have plenty of time to sweep and clean."

Otto introduced himself and said, "You may see me again, soon."

The young man introduced himself, "I am Johann Frick, I am glad to meet you, Otto, and by the way what do you do?"

Otto paused then said, "At the present nothing but I am preparing to make a dramatic change."

Otto then returned to the taxi and ordered the driver to take him back to the hotel.

Hans returned to the hotel very elated. When he located Otto he exclaimed, "I was greeted by the personnel manager of Lufthansa Airlines, Herr August Reinhardt, this morning and he assured me that I would begin a job as a co-pilot flying between Berlin and all the major cities on the continent, including London! I would first have to complete a mandatory training period then I would be presented with my 'wings'!"

Hans continued, "When Herr Reinhardt examined my record with the Luftwaffe, he called his entire staff to come to his office and he then introduced me as one of the famous 'Black Knights'! I met many former Luftwaffe officers now employed at Lufthansa Airlines who mobbed me for my autograph; Herr Reinhardt also wanted my autograph!"

Otto exclaimed, "Congratulations my friend, this will

bring joy to Elena and Max when you present them with the news, we have been invited to their home in Kreuzberg for dinner this evening."

Hans replied, "Yes, I know, the message was waiting for me when I returned a short time ago, hurry let's get ready!"

Max greeted Otto and Hans as they arrived at his home, Elena was busy with the housekeeper as the food was being prepared and served in the dining room.

Max told Elena, "Otto and Hans are here, come let them see my beautiful wife!"

Elena blushed as she greeted Otto and Hans, "Max is always saying something to make me blush, but welcome to our home, I have been waiting for this moment when Max' comrades would come to visit us, I wish Charles could have been here too."

After consuming the delicious roast beef, potatoes, and vegetables, everyone retired to the drawing room to exchange the news of the day.

Otto announced, "I saw a small coffee shop that I may purchase and convert into a nightclub with musicians and entertainers. The present owner is a young man who is content to eke out an existence in its present state. The news of the day is about Hans, I yield the floor to Hans!"

Hans declared, "The Black Knights are still famous after all these past years, once everyone at Lufthansa found out who I was they surrounded me, pushing papers in front of me asking for my autograph and insisting on me telling my war exploits. However, I have been accepted as an airline pilot, I will start out as a copilot after I complete my mandatory training."

After sipping the fine wine Hans continued, "I will be flying between Berlin and most of the major cities on the European continent and London!"

Max offered a toast to Hans on his appointment to Lufthansa Airlines; all raised their glasses to congratulate Hans.

Elena added, "Let us wish Otto success on his proposed nightclub and Charles with his bakery."

Again, all glasses were raised. At the conclusion of the dinner, Max drove his comrades back to their hotel.

Max said, "This has been a wonderful evening, we must do this more often." He then bid his comrades, "Auf Wiedersehn!"

Hans felt he was on top of the world now that he was flying again, no combat missions, no fear of being attacked by enemy fighters, peace at last.

Hans' training period was finally concluded and he received his 'wings', he was now a pilot for Lufthansa Airlines!

After months of flying to the major cities on the continent Hans received an assignment to fly to London, replacing the captain who had fallen ill. What irony, reminiscing Hans remembered many years before when he had flown over London's hostile skies and now his plane was descending peacefully into Heathrow Airport in this large beautiful city! After the passengers deplaned and the flight reports were completed Hans took a taxi to a local hotel to register, he had a two-day layover before returning to Berlin.

After refreshing himself, Hans decided to take a tour of the city. He hired a taxi and ordered the driver to take him to London's famous district of fashionable men's attire. After arriving in the area Hans decided to walk around and 'window shop'. Entering one of the stores Hans strolled through the aisles until a beautiful woman accidentally bumped into him.

Startled, Hans said, "I am so sorry, please forgive my clumsiness."

She demurely looked at him and said, "No, it was my fault, I was so engrossed in shopping for men's ties for my father that I did not see where I was going."

Hans replied, "Please allow me to help you, I am here to shop for clothes so I don't have to wear my uniform all the time."

For a moment, she stared at this dark handsome figure of a man, standing before her, trim in the crisp uniform of a flight captain.

She smiled at Hans and said, "I notice you have an accent, I believe it is German, what is your nationality?"

Hans replied, "I am German, I was born in Neundettelsau, a small farming town not far from Nuremberg. Let me introduce myself, I am Hans Thayer, flight captain of Lufthansa Airlines."

She introduced herself, "My name is Constance Brisbane, I am English and I live here in London."

Constance explained, "My father's birthday is approaching and I was shopping for a present for him."

Hans smiled as he replied, "I would be more than happy to assist you."

The couple strolled together through the aisles, smiling and talking about mundane things, oblivious to their surroundings. Hans was awestruck by Constance's beauty and her classic demeanor, Hans knew he had to see her again.

Hans said, "Constance, I wish to see you again, here is my card, my hub is located in Berlin and I live there also."

Constance thanked him and told him, "I will call you. I must go now."

Hans and Constance walked from the store and he hailed a taxi for her, as she entered the taxi he said, "Auf Wiedersehn, this has been a very eventful day."

Constance replied, "Au Revoir, it has been such a pleasure for me too." The taxi then disappeared in the distance.

Hans returned to the store where he was met by one of the clerks who offered to assist him with his purchases. After he finished Hans went to his hotel and packed for his return trip to Berlin.

On the flight back to Berlin the copilot, Matt Braun, said, "Hans, you have been smiling ever since you came back to the airport, that smile seems frozen to your face, what happened, did you find a pot of gold?"

Hans replied, "Yes, you can say 'I found a pot of gold', I met the most beautiful girl in the world, and I hope to see her again!"

After the flight was completed, Hans returned to his Berlin apartment, thinking about Constance and wondering if he would ever see her again.

Chapter

XXVI

Otto's Dream, the Creation of
the 'Black Knights Club'

Otto negotiated a partnership with Johann Frick for the coffee shop. Otto told Johann of his plans for expansion and the hiring of bands and singers of all musical styles. Johann listened intently, with the attention a young pupil gives to his professor. Otto hired carpenters and electricians to remodel the coffee shop, giving it a stage with elaborate lighting and a sound system to surround the customers with music.

As the work on the coffee shop progressed, Otto expressed the need for the hiring of qualified servers and bartenders to accommodate the many anticipated customers.

Johann said, "I will contact people my parents dealt with before the War, some of them still come here for coffee and conversation."

Otto said, "Good, I have seen some very good musicians gather in the park playing for handouts from passersby, I believe they would be happy to play before an appreciative audience here at our establishment."

The residents in the immediate neighborhood noticed the activity at the coffee shop and made inquiries as to its future, many expressing their approval of its conversion to an establishment that would supply music and entertainment.

Johann asked, "What will the name of our place be when we open for business?"

Otto exclaimed, "The 'Black Knights Club', I have been dreaming of this for a long time! I announced at the park that there would be auditions, beginning next week. Soon we will be booking major bands and performers!"

Johann shared Otto's enthusiasm, exclaiming, "I can hardly wait!"

As the weeks passed Otto and Johann auditioned many artists, picking out the most talented for opening night. Johann was able to recruit the necessary employees after interviewing the many applicants. After the completion of the remodeling, the announcement of 'Opening Night' was made in the entertainment newspapers citywide.

Otto notified his comrades of the 'Opening Night', only Elena and Max stated they would be able to attend. Hans was scheduled to fly from Budapest to Paris that weekend. Charles' bakery was in the final stages of construction, and Charles' presence was needed at the site. Both Hans and Charles sent their regrets.

The Opening Night was a gala affair with many of the local artists attending along with patrons from other sections of the city. The size of the crowd pleased both Otto and Johann. When Elena and Max arrived, Otto warmly greeted them and led them to a special booth he had reserved for them.

Otto introduced Johann to Elena and Max stating, "This is the young man who had owned this coffee shop before it became the 'Black Knights Club'."

Johann expressed his desire to serve Elena and Max personally. Johann related to them that Otto was an exceptional person.

Max thought to himself that indeed, Otto was an exceptional person, able to do anything! He told Otto, "I am truly amazed at your talents, so diverse, your opening night just adds to your successes! Otto I am so proud of you, my dear comrade, I must tell Hans and Charles of your Opening Night success!"

The next morning Otto and Johann conferred on the future of the club. Otto suggested that he would take trips to Paris and London to observe the operations of the small clubs and incorporate some of their ideas into the operation of the 'Black Knights Club'.

Johann exclaimed, "Otto, you are an amazing man, I realize you have said very little about your life but as your partner I need to know, please tell me more about you!"

Otto explained, "During the War, I became famous within the military, I am a former Luftwaffe fighter squadron commander, I received many awards and honors, but now that I am a civilian I wish to lead a quiet peaceful life and pursue my ambitions as a music producer."

Stunned, Johann replied, "Remarkable, carry on with your ambitions my friend, I am very fortunate to have you as a partner."

During the next months, the 'Black Knights Club' became a haven for unknown artists and entertainers who wished to showcase their talents. Every now and then, a famous singer or musician would visit the club and join in performing with the house band.

One night, a famous Parisian singer visited the club, known throughout the world as 'The Little Swallow', EDITH PIAF! Edith Piaf ordered her manager to locate the club's owner and have him come to her table. Her manager escorted Otto to her table, Otto stared at her in disbelief, "Welcome to the 'Black Knights Club' Madame Piaf!" he exclaimed, "What an honor!"

The petite Madame Piaf replied, "I am on a European

concert tour at this time and I stopped here in Berlin for a much needed rest between engagements. My avant garde friends suggested that I stop by your club and enjoy myself and relax, so here I am."

Otto assured her, "We will make your visit a most enjoyable one, I will have one of our waiters take care of you and your party immediately."

Otto summoned Johann and told him about the celebrity who was visiting the club. Johann exclaimed, "Otto, Madame Edith Piaf! Unbelievable!"

Otto took Johann to her table and introduced him, "Madame Piaf, if it were not for this young man, this club would not exist, he is my partner."

The word spread throughout the area that Edith Piaf was at the 'Black Knights Club', the club became crowded in a very short time. Otto and Johann struggled to keep the autograph seekers from overwhelming Madame Piaf with their requests. Finally, Otto and Johann were able to restore order.

Madame Piaf said, "Otto and Johann, both of you are such wonderful hosts, if your little orchestra can play one of my favorite songs, 'Tu Es Partout', then I will sing it for you."

Otto leaped to the stage and announced, "Our renowned guest wishes to sing for us, let me present, MADAME EDITH PIAF!"

After the applause and cheers died down the orchestra began playing, Madame Piaf sang with the passion that brought tears to the eyes of many in the audience. At the conclusion of her song, she bowed and thanked everyone for receiving her so warmly.

Madame Piaf told Otto, "Your club reminds me of my beginning, I started singing in a small club similar to this."

Madame Piaf and her entourage soon departed, again thanking Otto and Johann for a wonderful evening. After closing, Otto and Johann celebrated by opening a bottle of champagne, the 'Black Knights Club' became known throughout Berlin after this night.

Chapter

XXVII

Charles and His Bakery,
A Business Venture Come True

Charles' bakery supplied his parents' café with bread and pastries in addition to the increased business coming from the rising reputation of Charles' elaborate cakes for special occasions.

One afternoon a distinguished looking man entered Charles' bakery and introduced himself, "I am Josef Mintz, the Generaldirektor of the House of von Hoffensberg, here is my card. I wish to commission you to bake the bread and pastries for a special dinner being prepared by the Baroness von Hoffensberg."

Charles replied, "I shall be honored to bake for the Baroness von Hoffensberg."

Herr Mintz continued, "I have prepared a list of what the Baroness wants for her menu, any details that need to be worked out please contact me at once." Herr Mintz then left Charles' bakery.

Charles looked over the list and mused to himself, "This menu looks like something from the nineteenth century, when nobility ruled Europe; I have to do some research in preparing these ancient recipes."

Charles consulted with his father, Francois, seeking his knowledge of the old recipes for some of the pastries listed. Francois referred Charles to an old friend, Heinrich Dieter, who once had a bakery before the War but had since retired.

Charles visited his father's friend, Heinrich, and the two bakers, one from a bygone era, and the other, young and eager, discussed baking techniques into the evening hours. Charles returned to his bakery feeling energized by the knowledge he obtained from Heinrich and planned the most elaborate pastry combinations one could imagine.

Charles contacted Herr Mintz and notified him the breads and pastries were ready for delivery. Herr Mintz arrived in a limousine at Charles' bakery shortly thereafter.

Charles informed Herr Mintz, "I always accompany my special orders to their destination, it is my custom."

Herr Mintz replied, "But of course, I understand. I will introduce you to the Baroness, I am sure she would be pleased to meet you, the artist who prepared her treats."

Arriving at the von Hoffensberg Estate, Charles supervised the handling of the bakery goods from the limousine to the kitchen area, where the Baroness was anxiously waiting.

Herr Mintz brought Charles to the Baroness. He announced, "Baroness von Hoffensberg, this is Herr Charles Toulon, esteemed baker who has prepared the breads and pastries for your dinner!"

The Baroness stated, "Herr Toulon, I am so impressed by the beauty of the display of these pastries, some from very old recipes passed down through generations of the von Hoffensberg clan, I can hardly wait to taste them."

Charles assured her, "Baroness, I also brought samples for you to taste, I did not want you to have any doubt about what I had prepared for you and your guests."

Giggling, the Baroness said, "You have made me so happy, I know the Baron will be pleased also. Herr Mintz I want you to add a bonus to Herr Toulon's bill."

Herr Mintz replied, "Of course, Baroness von Hoffensberg."

Herr Mintz then had Charles driven back to his bakery.

The local newspapers carried the story of the von Hoffensberg dinner in detail; the affair was described as a huge success with special emphasis given on the pastries, prepared by the Toulon Bakery. Charles bought extra copies of the newspapers and mailed them to his fellow comrades.

Charles' business steadily grew, necessitating him to add more bakers and support staff. One day he received a surprise visitor, his former wingman, Ernst Schiller. After the two former fighter pilots warmly greeted each other Ernst said, "Charles my friend, I was released from captivity two years ago, Hugo and Rolf were released also, I have no news on the fate of Max' rear gunner, Erik Streicher."

Charles said, "Ernst my friend, where have you been staying, what have you been doing since being repatriated?"

Ernst replied, "Travelling and more travelling, working odd jobs, it seems there is an abundance of accountants everywhere, that was what I studied at school but I have yet to find a job in that profession."

Charles exclaimed, "You have shown up at the right time, I need an accountant, I don't have time to keep books and bake at the same time! Please stay and give me a helping hand!"

Ernst said, "Thank you, thank you, my prayers have been answered."

Charles inquired, "Ernst, what about your parents?"

Ernst replied, "They were killed in an air raid while visiting relatives in Dresden in 1945."

After a moment of silence, Charles said, "I am so sorry for you and I am so very fortunate, my parents are still alive and we still have the café."

Ernst exclaimed, "I am so happy for you, but now that I am your employee, we will continue to live and enjoy life as it is given to us. I weep no more and I want no one to weep for me!"

Charles took Ernst to the café and introduced him to his parents, he announced to the patrons, "Attention everyone, this is my former wingman, Ernst Schiller, I thought we would never meet again, but here he is! He is now my accountant and I want us all to welcome him!"

Every one shouted, "Welcome! Welcome Ernst Schiller!"

Charles mother told Ernst, "Sit down and have something to eat." She then gave him the menu.

Ernst told Charles, "I cannot express myself, all of this hospitality is overwhelming."

Charles answered, "This is the way we are in Saarbrucken, get used to it!"

Chapter

XXVIII

The Career of a Lufthansa
Flight Officer, A Very Happy Hans

A Lufthansa Airbus 300 taking off for a flight to America being flown by Chief Flight Captain Hans Thayer.

Hans received a promotion to Chief Pilot at Lufthansa Airlines. His routes were expanded to include trips to America. Otto and Max met at the 'Black Knights Club' to plan a celebration for Hans.

"These past years have been good to us", Max related, "Your club is the talk of the town, you are constantly meeting celebrities and becoming famous at producing good, quality shows. Charles' bakery business has grown to the extent that he has established bakeries in Paris and London and I am now one of the chief engineer designers at the Krupp Werks, but most of all I have a wonderful wife and two growing children, a son and a daughter."

Otto concurred, "You are absolutely right, but never let your guard down, the Russians are closing off their section of Berlin, I noticed they have erected a barbed wire fence separating their zone from the American, British, and French zones and I understand from my sources that they plan to erect a permanent concrete fence."

"I know", Max related, "Our good friend, General Tremirov, now retired, keeps me informed on the latest developments from his sources."

That evening Hans came to the club wearing his new uniform, he was greeted by Otto and directed to one of the special VIP booths. Max and Elena arrived shortly thereafter and joined in.

Otto exclaimed, "Hans, I have a treat for all of us, Charles is here in Berlin and is on his way here! I did not say anything until I was sure he arrived, he is staying at our favorite hotel, the Hotel Continental!"

When Charles entered the club all pandemonium

broke out, Johann announced, "Charles is here! Charles is here! The Black Knights were reunited once again!"

Charles gave Hans a 'bear hug' and said, "Congratulations my very good friend, you are flying for all of us! I miss soaring through the skies every now and then but then I return to my reality and bake my cakes!" Everyone enjoyed a hearty laugh. Otto said, "Charles, you should have become a comedian! I can use you in my show!"

The evening progressed and all enjoyed a good time. Hans was recognized and congratulated by many of the patrons, former Luftwaffe officers who regularly frequent the 'Black Knights Club'.

Elena asked Max, "What happened to the English girl that had Hans so smitten?"

Max replied, "Hans read in one of the London papers that she was engaged to a former RAF flyer and Hans stopped the correspondence between the two, he never mentioned her anymore."

A special cake from the Toulon Bakery was delivered to the club. Charles carefully removed it from the box and presented it to Hans. Everyone in the club raised their glasses as Charles delivered a special toast to Hans.

The festivities gradually concluded, the band played a rousing rendition of 'Flieger Sind Sieger' and anyone who knew the victory song of the Luftwaffe joined in the chorus.

Hans thanked everyone and announced, "My friends and comrades, I am planning my first trip to America, I will be landing in New York City. Now I must depart, I bid everyone Auf Wiedersehn!"

Hans' fellow Black Knights embraced him as he left the club.

The following week a large sleek Airbus took off from Berlin's Templehof Airdrome with Hans at the controls, heading to America! Hans had dreamed of this day, now it was a reality. After many hours, Hans brought the plane to a landing at JFK Airport, New York City. After his passengers deplaned Hans and his copilot were taken to the Lufthansa terminal office to check in and submit their logs.

The Lufthansa manager greeted Hans and introduced himself, "I am Anthony Smith, welcome to America Captain Thayer, my staff arranged accommodations for you during your lay-over. You will be staying at one of the first class hotels in Manhattan; one of my staff has volunteered to be available at your disposal during your layover, his name is Dennis McCoy, he is a young man in his twenties."

Hans thanked the manager, after Hans met Dennis McCoy the two left in a company car for the trip to Manhattan.

Hans queried, "Where do you live, Dennis?"

Awestruck, Dennis answered, "I live in Long Island, Captain Thayer, but I know my way around the city."

Hans replied, "After I go to my hotel and freshen up I want you to take me to Harlem, I have heard so much about it, I also want to go where I can hear 'jazz' music, come back and pick me up at 7:00PM."

Dennis exclaimed, "Yes Sir!"

As Dennis drove away from the hotel, he thought to himself, "I cannot believe what I just saw, a Black pilot, and a captain in command no less, flying for Lufthansa! He also has a thick German accent! I cannot believe it!"

Dennis returned at 7:00PM, Hans was waiting in the lobby of the hotel, wearing a suit and tie for eveningwear.

Hans said, "I see you are punctual, I like that, I am ready to see the New York sights."

Excitedly, Dennis asked, "Sir, I do not wish to intrude on your private life but, where were you born?"

Hans replied, "I was born in the little town of Neundettelsau, Germany, my parents are farmers, and to satisfy your curiosity, yes, I have an African father, he was born in Togoland. I could see in your face that you thought I was from another planet." Hans then broke into uncontrollable laughter. Dennis joined him in more uncontrollable laughter.

Hans inquired, "Are there many Black airline pilots here in America?"

Dennis answered, "Very few, Sir, some are with the major airlines, in some cases, former pilots that were in the War, they were known as the Tuskegee Airmen."

Hans replied, "There are very few Black pilots in Germany too, I flew in a flying circus before the War and then I became a fighter pilot in the Luftwaffe for the entire War, from the beginning to the end."

Dennis stared at Hans, speechless for a moment, he then exclaimed, "The Luftwaffe! Wow! Unbelievable!"

Hans said, "Enough, Dennis! Calm down and show me the sights of New York City."

As Dennis was driving toward Harlem, Hans thought to himself, "What a beautiful city, so many people of many different races, so much diversity. Now I am beginning to see more people of African ancestry as we continue to drive, we must be approaching Harlem."

Dennis said enthusiastically, "Captain Thayer, this is 125th Street, the main street in Harlem, see the Apollo Theatre over there, they always have good shows there, the top Black orchestras perform there, the top Black entertainers perform there, the Apollo is one of New York's top attractions! I will take you to one of the clubs where we can hear good jazz music."

Hans reflected, "Otto should be here to see this, I will tell him about Harlem when I see him again."

Dennis took Hans to a club where the music could be heard coming from inside, filling the street with the sounds of jazz emitting from the horns of musicians, playing from the depths of their souls. Hans and Dennis were seated at a table near the bandstand.

Dennis said, "I frequent this club almost every weekend, they always have some of the top musicians playing here. I will introduce you to the manager, Freddie; he is coming over to our table."

Freddie greeted Dennis, "How are you doing Dennis, who's your friend?"

Dennis said, "Freddie, this is Captain Hans Thayer of Lufthansa Airlines, he is here on a layover. He wanted to see Harlem and listen to good jazz, I brought him here to see and hear the best."

After the introduction, Freddie asked Hans, "Why are you talking with that funny sounding accent and did Dennis say you are an airline pilot for Lufthansa?"

Hans replied, "My English is good but my accent is still prominent, I am German and I will always have an accent, and yes, I am an airline pilot for Lufthansa."

Freddie responded, "Forgive my ignorance, I meant no harm, welcome to the club! Some of the musicians from the Count Basie band are here tonight, relaxing and playing, they have a gig at the Apollo Theatre tomorrow so they are keeping loose. I will send one of my waitresses over to take care of you and my buddy, Dennis, have a good time, I must circulate." Freddie then melted into the crowd.

Hans told Dennis, "You do the talking; I will keep quiet unless I have an important point to make."

Dennis said, "Yes Sir!"

One of the patrons overheard the conversation between Hans and Freddie and came over to Hans' table.

He introduced himself, "My name is Garnett Jenkins, did I hear you say that you are an airline pilot for Lufthansa?"

Hans replied, "Yes Sir, you heard me say that."

Garnett Jenkins explained, "During the War I was a fighter pilot, I flew with the 'Red Tails', the 332nd Fighter squadron, but at the present I am a New York City Transit employee, driving one of the subway trains, how did you get a job flying for Lufthansa? That is a German airline."

Dennis interrupted, "Captain Thayer IS German, not American, he was hired in his native country."

Garnett expressed surprise, "You are the first Black German I have ever seen, I was stationed in Europe for two years after the War and two years during the War and I never saw a Black German, not man, not woman, nor child!"

Hans explained, "We Black Germans are very rare indeed, when I served in the Luftwaffe, I got to know only three other Black German Luftwaffe officers during the entire War, we became known as the 'Black Knights'."

Dumbfounded, Garnett asked, "You were a Luftwaffe pilot? We never heard of any Luftwaffe pilots being anything other than pure Aryan Germans."

Hans stated, "I know, a few years ago my comrades and I were told by an important person that as far as the Western Alliance was concerned, WE DID NOT EXIST! I understand why you are stunned by this revelation."

Garnett asked, "Do you have anything with you to prove you were once a Luftwaffe Officer?"

Hans replied, "Yes, I still carry my old military identification as a memento to my daring impetuous youth, when I lived every day as if it was my last."

Hans retrieved his military ID from his wallet and showed it to Garnett, Hans also showed Garnett his pilot's license, indicating he was a Chief Flying Officer for Lufthansa Airlines. After a long silence, Garnett exclaimed, "Unbelievable! Where did you fight?"

Hans related, "The Battle of France, the Battle of

Britain, and finally the Battle for Russia!"

Garnett eagerly asked, "Did any of you fight against the United States Air Force when we were bombing your homeland?"

For a moment, Hans stared ahead in silence with a blank look, and then replied, "Regrettably, no, we were preoccupied with the Russians!"

Garnett stated, "I know my question may have seemed insensitive but I needed to know, the idea of men of African descent battling each other is also a very sensitive issue."

Hans assured Garnett, "I understand your point and I agree with you in principle but I must tell you, I would have fought against you to the death if I had fought against the Western Alliance instead of Russia! However, as far as my knowledge of the War, and information I have from other sources since the War, combat between us warriors of African descent never occurred!"

Dennis suggested to both men, "Gentlemen, the War is over, let us listen to this great music!"

Both Hans and Garnett agreed, and with Dennis joining in their conversation, they sat back and enjoyed the music. Hans looked about the club, observing couples dancing, others as if in a trance as the music played on. Hans expressed his approval of Dennis bringing him to Harlem. Hans, with his impeccable appearance and the self-assured aura he projected, made him the center of attraction to the many female patrons of the club. Soon Hans found himself surrounded by these admirers, inquiring to gather any information they could about him, Hans eagerly complied.

Hans whispered to Dennis, "These Black women are so beautiful, it is so unbelievable, I wish I could take them all back to Berlin with me! I must admit, I have never seen this many Black people at one time in my life, so many different hues! In Germany during my early childhood, the only Black person I ever saw or knew was my father! After the War I saw some American Black soldiers stationed in Berlin and Nuremberg, but that was the extent of it!"

Dennis reminded him, "Whenever your trips bring you back to back to America I will expand the tour of New York City to show you other neighborhoods and their unique culture, for example, near Harlem there is East Harlem with their Spanish culture and a different sound of music altogether, New York City has a wealth of diversity."

Hans exclaimed, "This is such a treat, I am looking forward to many more trips! Now I must return to my hotel, I have to report to the office tomorrow morning and plan for my return trip."

Hans told Garnett, "I enjoyed our conversation and I hope to see you again and perhaps I may meet some of your comrades, I must prepare for my return trip to Berlin so I wish you and all of these beautiful ladies 'Auf Wiedersehn'."

Hans and Dennis departed, leaving these citizens of Harlem awestruck!

The next morning Dennis picked Hans up from his hotel and as the two drove to JFK Airport, they reminisced about the trip to Harlem, Hans' adventure at an all-Black nightclub and the wonderful music. Arriving at the Lufthansa flight office they were greeted by the terminal manager, Anthony Smith.

"How were the accommodations, Capt. Thayer?"

"Very good, I am looking forward to many more trips to your fair city. I thank you for having Dennis show me around, he is a very capable young man."

After finishing his preparations, Hans caught the shuttle bus to his plane, there he met an old friend, Matt Braun. The two warmly greeted each other, Hans stated, "I understand you are to be my copilot on the return trip, what a turnaround, just a few years ago I was your copilot, mein Gott!"

Matt replied, "It is a pleasure to fly with you Hans, I knew you would become a chief pilot one day."

The large plane rose gracefully into the heavens, speeding effortlessly across the Atlantic Ocean below. The hours passed then the western portion of the continent came into view, Hans announced over the loudspeaker, "The coast is ahead, we shall be home soon."

Approaching the Berlin Templehof Airdrome, the plane descended peacefully to a smooth landing.

Chapter

XXIX

Otto's Emergency Trip Back
to Africa

A messenger delivered a telegram to the 'Black Knights Club'. Johann received it and noticed it was addressed to Otto; Johann went immediately to the office and handed it to Otto. After reading it Otto told Johann, "I have to go to Cameroon at once, my mother has summoned me. I will be gone for an undetermined amount of time, now I must make my flight arrangements."

Otto then hurriedly left the club. Johann notified Max and Hans of Otto's hasty departure to Cameroon.

"I do not know the reason for Otto's haste; I do know the telegram was from his mother, it must have been very important." Johann related to Max and Hans.

After his flight landed at the Douala airport, one of the Elders met Otto and transported him directly to the Queen's residence. Arriving at the Queen's estate Otto hurriedly went to the main conference room where his mother, the Queen, was waiting. There she stood, in all her regal splendor, her soft silvery hair framing her beautiful face, smiling as she looked at her son as he rushed into the room.

After a long embrace, Queen Tikwana told Otto, "Your great-uncle, Chief Umgato, is very ill, he is very old and weak and not expected to recover. He has called for an emergency meeting of all the Elders; I am to preside over the meeting, now that you are here we can proceed immediately."

That evening Otto met with the Chief, lying in his bed with his eyes partially closed. Chief Umgato turned his head toward Otto as Otto entered the room.

"Uncle Umgato, I am here to be at your side, what would you have me do?"

Chief Umgato raised himself on one elbow and motioned Otto to come closer, he replied, "There will be an election for the next Chief of the Ubo tribe, I am about to join my ancestors very soon and sit beside my brother King Nkuno, all elders must be present to vote, your mother will preside over the election process. I have already submitted your name to become the next Chief; you are our most revered warrior, having proven yourself in battle!"

"I am so honored, my Chief, but by the laws of our constitution, the Chief must be a 'pure' Ubo descendant, from an Ubo father and an Ubo mother."

"Enough! Otto, I am well aware of the law but there are extenuating circumstances in your case and I have argued your case before the Elders! Some are willing to amend the law so that those who deserve the recognition for their deeds and valor will be so honored, and of course there are those who will stick to the law as is and refuse to budge no matter what argument is presented to them!"

After his meeting with Chief Umgato, Otto returned to the conference room and told his mother of the meeting.

Queen Tikwana replied, "Yes my son, I am aware of your great-uncle's request, his dreams are far into the future, maybe someday there will come a change but not now, maybe even a woman can become a Chief instead of just a Queen. The election will be in a fortnight."

Otto retired to his quarters and thought to himself, "The same law that was in effect during the last régime in my 'other' country, only now it is the reverse, what irony!"

The Elders held a meeting with council members and requested Otto's appearance. Otto accepted, two of the Elders who were in favor of him becoming the next Chief presented him before the council. Otto thanked all the Elders for the invitation. Otto acknowledged that the recommendation of his becoming the next Chief of the Ubo tribe was a challenge to the ancient laws of their constitution and that he would accept the Chiefdom only if the vote was unanimous. This move by Otto gained the respect of all the Elders and council members and he received a standing ovation.

On the fortnight, the day of the election, the ballots were submitted and later counted. The decision to amend the law to allow a person other than a 'pure' Ubo adult, the son of an Ubo father and of an Ubo mother, to become a Chief of the Ubo tribe was soundly defeated by an overwhelming majority.

Otto went to Chief Umgato to give him the news of the election. His mother, who was at the bedside of Chief Umgato said, "Chief Umgato has started his journey to the ancestral retreat where he will be reunited with his brother and all the other Kings and Chiefs who have passed this way."

When Queen Tikwana stood and raised her hand, the drums resounded and reverberated throughout the land with the cries of the populace chanting, "Hail to the Chief! Long live the Chief!" Otto stood at attention and saluted the passing of his great-uncle.

There would be one week of mourning and the Elders would be meeting during this time to elect a new Chief from among themselves. Since Otto was an honorary Elder, he participated in the voting process.

After the election of the new Chief and the inauguration there was rejoicing followed by the rituals that included performers, seemingly in a trance as they danced themselves into a frenzy, their voices singing the stories of ancient battles fought and their voices rising to a crescendo telling the stories of the great victories that were won! Otto was mesmerized as he witnessed these performances, he would later relate how the music cast a hypnotic spell over him.

The day came when Otto came to his mother and announced he was returning to Berlin, during their meeting he reassured her that his visits would be more frequent. After they embraced Otto's escort arrived to transport him to the Douala Airport. After boarding his plane Otto took his seat and reflected on his experiences, Otto silently thought, "What a beautiful country, I will surely miss it, I vow to return."

Chapter

XXX

The Return to Berlin and News
About
Other Comrades from the Past

Johann met Otto at the airport on his arrival back in Berlin. Otto discussed bringing native singers and dancers from Africa to the club.

"The music is so moving Johann, it is infectious and intoxicating! Your body wants to move, your feet want to dance!" Otto exclaimed, "We will be the first to introduce the African culture to Berlin through our club!"

"That is the way Hans described the music he heard when he visited a nightclub in Harlem when he was in New York City, he called the music, 'Jazz'," Johann replied, "he said you should go to America and hear it for yourself, he said you cannot sit still when you are listening to it."

"Johann, we have an unlimited future in music presentation at our club, I have been thinking of expanding the club to accommodate the crowds we have been attracting. We can renovate that abandoned factory building across the street. Find out who the owners are and negotiate a deal, we have enough capital to buy that property!"

Excitedly, Johann exclaimed, "I will take care of that immediately!"

Otto thought, "There are some jazz musicians already here in Europe, mainly in Paris and London, I will see and hear them before I make my trip to America."

Otto received a call from Max, "I have news for all of us, Elena and I will be at the club tonight. I understand Hans had a flight to Budapest and Charles is busy with his baking but we will be there in our favorite booth at about 8:00PM."

Otto replied, "It will be so good to see the both of you, I also have much to tell you."

That evening Max and Elena arrived at the 'Black Knights Club', Otto greeted them and directed them to their favorite booth located just off the stage.

Max started the conversation, "I have located my former gunner, Erik Streicher, he was repatriated over two years ago and is working in a furniture factory in Regensburg. Our good friend, Retired Gen. Tremirov found him along with Hugo and Rolf through his connections. Hugo returned to his parent's estate and is in the process of restoring it. Some ferocious battles were fought on the property during the war and everything was destroyed, his parents were killed, nothing was left. While he was a prisoner of war the property was left unattended and deteriorated to nothing! Rolf was released with him and is now helping him rebuild, Rolf's family also perished during the war!"

"That is wonderful news, knowing that they survived the prison camps, I am sorry to hear about their families however." Otto then asked, "Have you contacted Erik?"

"No, not yet," Max replied, "I will go to Regensburg and meet him in person. I sent a telegram to his factory so he will know I am coming."

Otto then told Max and Elena of his experiences while in Cameroon. Otto also told of his plans to expand the club and bring the songs of Africa to the club.

"In addition I will bring American jazz music here too," Otto explained, "the Black Knights Club will be the talk of Berlin!"

"All of that is wonderful news," Max related, "I have more wonderful news, I have been offered a promotion and the company is moving Elena and I to Munich, I will be the new plant manager there! Our children are already enrolled in one of the premier schools in Munich."

Otto stated, "This calls for a celebration, too bad Charles and Hans are not here to join in. I will notify them of these events including the news about Erik, Hugo, and Rolf."

Chapter

XXXI

A Reassessment of One's Life and
Preparations for a Long Vacation,
America Here Come the Black Knights

When Hans returned to Berlin he was greeted with the news of Rolf Friedland, his wingman during the war, working on the restoration of the von Wassel Estate.

Hans asked Otto, "What are your plans concerning Hugo and Rolf?"

Otto said, "If you can get a break in your schedule I can arrange for us to go to the von Wassel Estate at once."

Hans stated, "I will make the necessary changes immediately."

Johann assured Otto the club business would continue smoothly while he took the emergency leave.

The von Wassel Estate is located east of the Hurtgen Forest near the town of Schmidt. When the train pulled into the station the townspeople, led by Hugo von Wassel and Rolf Friedland, greeted Otto and Hans like returning heroes. These two 'Black Knights' being reunited with their wingmen evoked cheers and tears from the endearing crowd.

Otto stared at Hans in amazement, "They still remember us after all of these years!"

Hans uttered, "This is beyond my comprehension, I have no words to explain this."

Hugo and Rolf drove Otto and Hans to the estate. Arriving, Otto and Hans observed the extent of the damage, they both uttered, "Unbelievable! Total devastation!"

Otto stated, "It would take a hundred years to clear away the rubble and rebuild unless you had the necessary heavy equipment. Hans and I will authorize the contractors to bring in whatever equipment that is necessary!"

A telegram arrived from Max and Charles. Otto read it aloud, "Max and Charles said there will be no limit on the expense to complete this project! We are united to restore the von Wassel Estate, no matter the cost!"

In a matter of days, bulldozers, graders, and dozens of other pieces of heavy equipment arrived and the work began immediately. Hugo tried to express himself and could find no words, Rolf was also speechless.

Hans told everyone present, "You, Hugo and Rolf, were an extension of Otto and me, there were countless times when you two were always present to save our lives, this is nothing compared to that!"

There followed a moment of silence.

Otto stood and said, "Hans and I must return to Berlin at once, we will keep abreast of the progress of the restoration, when the job is finished we will all rejoice!"

The return train ride was subdued as Otto and Hans were deep in their thoughts, as both reflected on the scenes of destruction they had witnessed.

After Otto and Hans arrived in Berlin, Otto offered Hans to have dinner at the club with him, Hans declined stating he had to go to Lufthansa Headquarters and set up his new schedule. Arriving at the club Otto was surprised to see Charles there.

Charles said, "Otto, I have been so involved with my bakery business that I have neglected my personal life, I must change. My parents are getting old and they are preparing to retire. The café is still operating but I do not know how much longer it will remain in the family, I cannot operate the café and conduct bakery business at the same time. I have to sell the café!"

"Charles, that is the price of success, look at me, I am juggling shows, auditioning new talent, booking proven talent and reaching out to famous acts to appear at the club, I do not have time to eat sometimes. Thank God I have Johann!"

Charles exclaimed, "I have many employees working for me, I have bakeries in Paris and London, in addition to my flagship bakery here in Germany, and I am exploring the possibility of opening bakeries in America, the opportunities are boundless!"

Otto applauded, "Charles you will soon be a rich man, congratulations!"

Charles lamented, "But, I have no life! At least you are around people every day and night; I am surrounded by beautiful pastries! Occasionally I will dine with the Baroness but she is old enough to be my mother!"

After uncontrolled laughter, Otto suggested, "Charles, take a cruise, go to Africa, go to America, your staff can get along without you for a while, take some time off, enjoy yourself!"

"Otto, you are right! I will take time off; I will stay here in Berlin for a week, I will be at the Hotel Continental! Tonight I will dine here at the club and enjoy the show!"

After Charles left to go to the hotel Otto mused, "I have no life either but I am surrounded by beautiful girls instead of 'beautiful pastries', which does make a difference."

Otto retired to his apartment and took a much needed rest.

That evening a refreshed Charles came to the club, Johann directed him to a booth located near the stage.

Johann told Charles, "Otto will be here soon, he usually arrives about 7:00 to 7:30PM. I understand you will be dining here tonight, I will send the waitress over."

Otto arrived and joined Charles; the waitress came to the booth with the menu.

Otto suggested, "We imported salmon for today's menu, the chef will broil it to perfection and garnish it with vegetables, there is also our standard, the roast beef and boiled potatoes with vegetables."

Charles replied, "I will have what you have, they both sound good."

Otto placed the order for the salmon.

Charles queried, "What condition was the von Wassel Estate in? I understand there was damage everywhere, the house was nothing but a pile of rubble."

Otto replied, "The damage was extensive, but the main problem was that the property had not been maintained over the course of the years after the war. One could tell that there had been heavy fighting in the area, many destroyed vehicles and rusted tanks littered the grounds everywhere."

Johann approached the two with a message from Hans. The message enclosed a schedule of Hans' flights for the foreseeable month. In the message Hans stated he was preparing for his flight to Paris and would return in two days, his next flight would be to America, JFK Airport.

"I am sorry I will miss Hans, I will be back to my pastries by the time he returns." Charles lamented.

Otto retorted, "Charles, you should book a flight to America, I know Hans is happy too about his flight to New York, he was very excited about it after his first visit. You should go, you need a change of scenery."

"Soon, my friend, soon." Charles replied.

The Master of Ceremonies jumped to the stage and announced, "Showtime! The Black Knights Club is proud to announce we are bringing to you one of the top blues singers from America, Johnny Lee Hooker and His Orchestra!"

Otto told Charles, "Sit back and enjoy the show, Johnny Lee Hooker is one of the most famous of the 'blues singers' from America, he is the present rage of the Paris night clubs."

After the performance, Johnny Lee Hooker came over to Otto's booth, he noticed Charles sitting there and commented, "Otto, Am I seeing another Black German in your booth?"

"Yes you are, I want you to meet my very good friend Charles Toulon, the greatest baker in all of Germany."

Charles and Johnny shook hands and exchanged the pleasantries of meeting each other. As the evening progressed, the conversation gravitated towards America, both Otto and Charles fielded endless questions to Johnny Lee Hooker, transfixed on every word as he described his life in America.

With the arrival of closing time, Johnny Lee Hooker and his band wrapped it up and bid Otto and Charles, "Au Revoir, we will meet again, I like your club."

After they left, Charles exclaimed, "You never cease to amaze me, Otto, it is like magic the way you get these big name acts to stop by this club from their regular gigs and get them to perform at least one show for you, you are truly amazing!"

With a chuckle Otto replied, "Give credit to Johann, he set this little show up when I was in Africa."

Charles noticed a group of people coming in the door and nudged Otto, "Otto look, some people of color coming in to the club, I believe they are Americans by the way they are dressed."

"I believe you are right Charles, they just missed the performance of one of their blues singers, but they will be pleased with the remainder of the entertainment."

Johann greeted the group of four men and four women. He brought them to Otto's booth, Otto and Charles stood up to greet them.

One of the men stepped forward and introduced himself, "I am Garnett Jenkins, from America and these are my friends and their wives also from America. I met an airline pilot who flew for Lufthansa, he mentioned this club, 'The Black Knights'. The pilot identified himself as Hans Thayer, do you know him?"

Otto laughed and said, "Yes, we know him, he is as close as a brother to both Charles and me, he told us of his visit to Harlem in New York City and how he met a former black American fighter pilot and the lively conversation he became engaged in with this man. Are you the one?"

"Yes, I am the one. These other gentlemen with me are also former fighter pilots, we were known as the Tuskegee Airmen, or 'Red Tails', we flew with the 332nd Pursuit Squadron, United States Air Force. We saw action in Italy as well as Germany. Hans told me that if I ever visited Berlin to be sure to go to the 'Black Knights Club' and meet his comrades-in-arms."

Charles exclaimed, "What a surprise, we heard of you as the war was drawing to a close but as fate would have it, we were preoccupied with the Russians!"

Garnett explained, "We never knew of the existence of any black German Luftwaffe pilots, my friends here still find it hard to believe, I told them Hans had produced his Luftwaffe identification but they still could not imagine there were any black German fighter pilots."

Otto reassured the group, "There were four of us in the same fighter group, and I was a squadron commander! Charles here was the highest scoring fighter pilot 'ace' in our fighter wing with over two hundred and thirty victories, and Hans also had over two hundred victories!"

Garnett and his entourage were speechless and transfixed as Otto and Charles further explained their roles and the roles of Hans and Max during the Great War. Otto took the group on a tour of the club, showing the many pictures affixed to the walls with the Black Knights and their planes. Otto took them to his office and produced some of his log books, indicating the many missions he flew, he also displayed copies of his promotions and awards that included his Knight's Cross and his Iron Crosses, both 1st Class and 2nd Class.

Garnett exclaimed, "This is astonishing, an unknown chapter in history has been unveiled! Let us exchange addresses Otto, we must keep our lines of communication open. This visit to your club has been the highlight of our vacation! In addition to the tour of the club, the entertainment and food were excellent. We all thank you, Johann, and Charles for your generous hospitality."

After the group left the club Johann said, "I believe they all had a wonderful time, once they became relaxed I could see they were excited to be here."

Charles thought for a moment and said, "I think I will take a vacation in America, why don't you join me Otto, you need a change of pace too."

Otto replied, "I think I will."

Hans had a flight to Berlin from London with a two-day layover. When Otto and Charles met with Hans, they told Hans of their plans to vacation in America. Hans was delighted and said, "Wait until I schedule my vacation and the three of us can go together."

Otto told Hans of the visit to the club of a party of American Air Force veterans that included Garnett Jenkins, the former fighter pilot that Hans had met in a New York City nightclub.

Hans exclaimed, "Garnett did say he would come to the 'Black Knights Club' if he ever visited Berlin, I see he kept his word!"

Charles added, "We need a long vacation, we are in our mid forties and all we have to show for it is a life of fighting and working, at least Max is settled and has a family!"

Hans said, "We do have our careers and we have been successful, let us give thanks to God Almighty, there are still signs of ruin from the war everywhere!"

Otto replied, "Amen! I propose that instead of this being a vacation that we make this an extended tour of the United States of America!"

Hans said, "Splendid idea, I must tell Max of our planned trip to America."

Max invited the trio to come to Munich to see his new home before embarking on their planned trip. Max told his comrades, "I wish I could join you but the chance of me making an extended trip is far into the future now that I am in my new position as the manager of this huge plant."

Hans obtained a leave of absence; he had an itinerary developed by the Lufthansa Airlines for the trio to visit New York City, Chicago, Detroit, Las Vegas, Los Angeles, and Hollywood in addition to touring the heartland of America.

After bidding Auf Wiedersehn and Au Revoir to friends and families, Otto, Charles and Hans boarded their flight to America.

As their flight soared into the heavens, Hans commented, "How strange it is to have someone flying me instead of me flying them."

That brought a hearty chuckle from the trio.

One could not help but wonder about the future of the Black Knights and what new adventures awaited Otto, Charles and Hans as they flew into the uncertainties and opportunities this great country had to offer. The saga of the Black Knights continues...

The End of the Beginning...!

Glossary

Military Rank of the Luftwaffe (1935-1945)	
Luftwaffe Rank	U.S. Rank
Reichmarschall	None
Generalfeldmarschall	General of the Air Force
Generaloberst	General
General der Fleger	Lieutenant General
General der Fallschirmtruppe	Lieutenant General
Generalleutnant	Major General
Generalmajor	Brigadier General
Oberst	Colonel
Oberstleutnant	Lieutenant Colonel
Major	Major
Hauptmann	Captain
Oberleutnant	First Lieutenant
Leutnant	Second Lieutenant
Stabsfeldwebel	Chief Master Sergeant
Hauptfeldwebel	Senior Master Sergeant
Oberfeldwebel	Master Sergeant
Feldwebel	Technical Sergeant
Unterfeldwebel	Staff Sergeant
Unteroffizier	Sergeant
de:Stabsgefreiter	Corporal
Hauptgefreiter	Senior Ariman
Obergefreiter	Airman First Class
Gefreiter	Airman First Class
Flieger	Airman Basic